Adult Children Of Alcoholics In Treatment

Stephanie Brown, Ph.D.
Susan G. Beletsis, Ph.D.
Timmen L. Cermak, M.D.

Health Communications, Inc.
Deerfield Beach, Florida

Stephanie Brown, Ph.D.
Susan G. Beletsis, Ph.D.
Timmen L. Cermak, M.D.

Reprinted with permission from *International Journal of Group Psychotherapy* and *Focus on Women: Journal Of The Addictions And Health.*

Library of Congress Cataloging-in-Publication Data

Brown, Stephanie
    Adult children of alcoholics in treatment / Stephanie Brown, Susan
G. Beletsis. Timmen L. Cermak.
        p.   cm.
    Includes bibliographies.
    ISBN 1-55874-032-5
    1. Adult children of alcoholics — Mental health.   2. Group
psychotherapy.   I. Beletsis, Susan G., 1938-   . II. Cermak.
Timmen L. III. Title.
RC569.5.A29B76   1989   89-11131
616.86′1—dc20   CIP

Publisher: Health Communications, Inc.
             Enterprise Center
             3201 S.W. 15th Street
             Deerfield Beach, FL 33442

Cover design by Vicki Sarasohn

Dedication

To our clients, who have taught us what it means to "make real the past."

Contents

Introduction vii

1. Interactional Group Therapy With
    The Adult Children Of Alcoholics 1
    by Timmen L. Cermak, M.D. and
    Stephanie Brown, Ph.D.

2. A Developmental Framework For Understanding
    The Adult Children Of Alcoholics 19
    by Susan G. Beletsis, Ph.D. and
    Stephanie Brown, Ph.D.

3. The Development Of Family Transference
    In Groups For The Adult Children
    Of Alcoholics 43
    by Stephanie Brown, Ph.D. and
    Susan G. Beletsis, Ph.D.

Introduction

Until recently, children of alcoholics (CoAs) and adult children of alcoholics (ACAs or ACoAs) were not recognized as a legitimate population requiring education, intervention and treatment for the effects of growing up with an alcoholic parent in an alcoholic environment. The reality of parental alcoholism could not be known to these children and to the millions of adults who had grown up in the same circumstance. The reality was also unrecognized and unknown by the people who might have helped — doctors, nurses, educators, writers, reporters, grandparents, aunts and uncles.

In essence nobody knew, or rather, nobody *could* know. But then, through the popular media and a group of professionals dedicated to telling the truth, children of alcoholics and adult children of alcoholics were named and described and the collective denial was broken. The label named reality and thereby directed the focus of investigation, intervention and treatment attention to the source: understanding the impact of the alcoholism of a parent on a child's adjustment and development.

Several of us at the Stanford Alcohol Clinic were privileged to be a part of this new movement, as we named the population and developed clinical services, professional training and clinical research.

In 1977 I founded the Stanford Alcohol Clinic in the Department of Psychiatry at Stanford University. The structure of the clinic was new and quite different from alcohol treatment centers established in the decade of the '70s. In this outpatient clinic, with a traditional mental health structure, treatment was available to any person with any concern about alcohol or drugs — their own use or that of someone else. This broader structure vastly enlarged the range of individuals recognized as needing treatment and the scope and definition of what constituted treatment. Thus, the door was open for adult children of alcoholics to seek treatment as identified patients — separate from the alcoholic. The structure of the clinic facilitated the labeling of this population and also permitted spouses, friends, employers and other relatives to seek treatment for the consequences or impact of someone else's alcoholism or chemical dependence.

It was but a short next step to offer service specifically for adult children of alcoholics. In 1978 Dr. Timmen Cermak and I started our first long-term interactional therapy group for adult children of alcoholics, a group we called ACAs. Tim was a resident in psychiatry who had heard me lecture on children of alcoholics and was struck by the radically new perspective such an idea rendered. It was an entirely new and different door into alcoholism — not focused on the alcoholic, but on alcoholism and its impact on children and family. Tim was one of the first physicians to recognize that many, if not a majority, of mental health patients were children of alcoholics and to ask whether their emotional difficulties as adults were related to growing up with an alcoholic parent.

Tim and I formed our first group by word-of-mouth. It took eight months to get a core group of four women. Shortly, we added more (men and women) and after that we were never without a long waiting list.

During the first year of our work with this group, we both were struck by the central themes and the style and pattern of interactions that emerged. Tim took the lead in a closer inspection, reviewing the detailed summaries we had written for every group to verify these themes and outline their content and pattern. Our first paper, "Interactional Group Therapy with the Adult Children of Alcoholics," published in the *International Journal of Group Psychotherapy* in 1982, appears as the first article in this volume.

In addition to offering clinical services, the Stanford Alcohol Clinic was also a training and research center. Thus, over the next ten years, many more groups for Adult Children of Alcoholics would be offered by therapists who were in clinical training themselves. They were supervised by a core staff of Tim, myself and Dr. Susan Beletsis.

Susan joined the Alcohol Clinic as a psychologist in 1978 and offered the second long-term group for ACAs. Two groups made a real clinical service and a basis for comparison. All three of us were very interested in the content and themes of these groups and in theory development — how were ACAs similar to other psychiatric populations and how were they different and, in particular, what established theoretical frames would be useful in better understanding the ACA population.

With Susan's initiative, we tackled the theoretical question using Erikson's developmental theory as a guide for understanding the effects of parental alcoholism on the normal tasks of childhood development. Our paper, "A Developmental Framework for Understanding the Adult Children of Alcoholics," published by *Focus on Women, Journal of Addictions and Health*, is the second article in this volume.

At the same time that we were beginning our clinical research, the idea of children of alcoholics was catching fire at the grass roots level as a national and international social movement. Others around the country also had been labeling this population, offering services and asking pertinent and critical theoretical and research questions. It was clearly an idea whose time had come. Tim and I were part of this larger group which formed the National Association of Children of Alcoholics (NACoA) in 1982.

It is really quite phenomenal that some 28 million adults, unlinked only 10 to 12 years ago, now constitute an identified population, sharing the heritage and identity of having grown up with an alcoholic parent. The rapid development of the social movement has pushed the professional clinical and research communities to offer services for both young children and adults and to undertake formal research.

As a clinician and clinical researcher myself, I also developed a keen interest in group therapy and how the two fit together. To follow up this interest, Susan and I examined the process of the clinical phenomenon of transference within the ACA group. Because of the label ACA, we changed the term to "family transference," indicating the powerful link from parent to child and the impact of the family environment and family system dynamics on the developing child. That paper, "The Development of Family Transference in Groups for the Adult Children of Alcoholics," published in the *International Journal of Group Psychotherapy* in 1986, is the third and final article in this volume.

Tim, Susan and I continue to receive requests for these early papers as knowledge and interest about ACAs grows, so we decided to put them together in this book. Although clinical and theoretical in design and published originally for professionals, we believe they speak to and will be helpful to a much wider audience. We are grateful to Health Communications for publishing this work and to the original journals for permission to reprint.

Barely a decade old, children of alcoholics is now a maturing grass roots social movement and a legitimate clinical population. In addition to helping millions of individuals, this movement has had and will have a major effect on mental health and chemical dependency theory and practice as the reality of a child's experience is recognized to have a wide-ranging and profound impact on development.

Stephanie Brown

Interactional Group Therapy With The Adult Children Of Alcoholics

by Timmen L. Cermak, M.D.
and
Stephanie Brown, Ph.D.

In line with recent systems models of alcoholism (Stein-glass, Weiner, and Mendelson, 1971; Bowen, 1974; Ablon, 1976), we at Stanford Alcohol Clinic have been treating alcoholics in group and family settings, as well as using the more traditional individual approach. The disturbances seen in the family structure of the alcoholic inevitably affect other family members. Yet the need for individual or group treatment for family members has never been fully appreciated except as it has pertained to the treatment of the alcoholic. Our belief that the relatives of alcoholics are legitimate candidates for treatment in their own right, independent of the alcoholic, has been reinforced by ob-servations of psychiatrists at Stanford and therapists in practice in the community. According to those clinicians, many adults seeking treatment for a general psychiatric problem eventually mention an alcoholic parent in their backgrounds. Both patient and therapist have often failed to appreciate the significance of that early experience to the patient's subsequent adult development. On the basis of that experience, we felt that a dynamic interactional group, which was found helpful with alcoholic patients, might also benefit their now adult children.

This paper reports our clinical impressions, derived from a small number of patients. Final conclusions can be made only after controlled research studies have been under-taken. Nevertheless, we feel that publication of our pilot results is an integral step toward the realization of the required research.

Clinical Samples And Methods

We began our initial group with four women, all self-referred, ranging in age from 28 to 55. Subsequently, we added nine members, including four men. More than 20 additional adult children of alcoholics have been seen indi-vidually by us but are not referred to directly in this paper. As a result of national and local publicity about our pilot group, we now run four groups (30 members) and con-tinue to have a waiting list.

Each member was interviewed by one of the co-thera-pists to gather detailed information, to screen for severe psychopathology or inappropriate expectations that would contraindicate inclusion in the group, and to begin the inculcation of mores and values conducive to effective group work. A list of 10 items, labeled "group therapy criteria," was given to each prospective member at the time of the screening interview. The handout stressed the importance of honest interpersonal exploration, explained the unstructured style of group therapy, explicitly re-quested a nine-month commitment and acknowledged the stress and pain involved in participation in such a risk-taking forum. Led by a female-male co-therapy team, the group has met weekly for three years, with each session lasting one and a half hours. Written, editorialized sum-maries are made of each meeting and mailed to members within two days (Yalom, Brown, and Bloch, 1975).

Our approach to group therapy, presented elsewhere in relation to work with alcoholics (Yalom, 1974; Brown and Yalom, 1977), is patterned closely on the framework expli-cated by Yalom (1970).

Members decided to join the group for a variety of reasons. Although many children of alcoholics continue to deny the existence of parental alcoholism, even after hav-ing left their family of origin, those who joined our group had come to acknowledge the problem. Some joined as a statement of their commitment to face realities ignored by their families. Others joined with the hope of breaking their identification with the alcoholic parent and to face the consequent fear that their own alcoholism is inevitable. Several stated in their screening interviews that they saw their membership in the group as a means of prevention.

Members also joined to break a strong emotional tie to their families of origin. Many continue to feel responsible for the welfare of their parents and siblings, long into adulthood. As a result, they are unable to form primary attachments to their own families and feel tremendous problems with intimacy in their own closest relationships.

Many members experienced severe conflict at their decision to participate, guiltily viewing group membership as equivalent to abandoning their alcoholic parents.

Much study is required to uncover the factors that determine whether or not the child of an alcoholic will recognize and acknowledge the problem of alcoholism and subsequently be able to seek help. Though conflicted, frightened, and reluctant, our members demonstrated keen awareness and clarity about their reasons for joining.

One member was frightened by her rigid emphasis on behavior control with her two children. She found that she responded to her son's age-appropriate expressions of anger, tears and outrage, with absolute intolerance and frustration. Her son's sudden tantrums were reminiscent of her mother's uncontrolled mood changes when drinking, and both left her with a sense of inadequacy to comfort or pacify those who are dependent on her.

Clinical Observations

Our observations of the issues and dynamics that characterize group meetings could be condensed into one word, "control." Conflicts involving issues of control were pervasive and often were the context within which other issues concerning trust, acknowledgment of personal needs, responsibility, and feelings arose. In nearly all cases, the emergence of those separate issues was accompanied by preoccupation with the overriding conflicts regarding control. The concern with control was often the most significant source of anxiety.

The Issue Of Control

Concern with issues of control is manifested on both the interpersonal and the intrapsychic levels. The modality of group psychotherapy promotes sufficient interaction to arouse intense interpersonal conflict. For example, group members fear either that they tend to be too controlling of the meeting or that others have taken over. Silence on one member's part is frequently intended as a passive resistance to demands by others to speak. One member acknowledged remaining silent in order to control whether others have an opportunity to attend to her, value her, or reject her. Others confirmed that they felt controlled by those silences. A portion of a weekly summary illustrates this issue:

Sue acknowledged that she is very rigid about control. Most of the time in a group situation she sees that her choices are to be silent, alone, or withdrawn. To participate in the group is equal to being responsible for whatever happens and for the feelings and reactions of all the other members. Sue also controls her own level of feelings, often warding off emotion in herself because to feel for others is to become responsible for them. Sue cannot share her own feelings either, because that is tantamount to making others responsible for her. Thus it became clear that Sue's silence is the only choice she has.

Another member complained that the style of each member's speaking in turn (a predominant mode of interaction early in the group) silenced her. She felt overwhelmed by the perceived demand for her to continue speaking once she had started, and the aura of performing in the spotlight kept her from starting to speak at all. Uninterpretable expressions on the therapists' faces were perceived as threats, requests, or demands to speak more. Members avoided breaking silences for fear of being seen as too controlling. Constructive feedback is frequently seen as a command to change, as well as rejection. The written weekly summary has often been attacked for its power to have the last word, its tendency to wonder about members' motives, and its ability to make definite statements about group members. All those factors contribute to the members' dysphoric sense of being one down, exemplified by the following note from a summary:

After a number of weeks of discomfort and blank faces in response to Tim's question, members finally attacked him directly. They insisted they could not understand his style of questioning. They felt stupid in the eyes of other members because, since they couldn't understand the question, they could not know what was expected of them. They had spent their lives anticipating the "correct" response demanded by a particular individual or particular situation. Tim's lack of clarity now made them feel like failures.

On an intrapsychic level, conflict is created when a part of one's self attempts to control the whole. Each member expressed strong opinions as to the relationship between affect and his or her estimated level of self-control. All feelings are seen as bad because affect is experienced as a lack of control. Therefore, members use denial, suppression, and repression liberally in an effort to keep tight reins on the outward expression and inward awareness of emotions. All acknowledged problems in the area of expressing anger, which they avoid by projecting a facade of having themselves under control. One member controls her feelings of sadness and anger by actively suppressing them, lest they begin to achieve expression and escalate out of control. She fears that, if she permitted herself to throw one plate out of frustration, nothing would stop her from throwing 30 plates.

The projected image of being in full control of oneself was frequently acknowledged to be a facade by group members. Yet, that behavioral facade was felt to be of considerable importance for both interpersonal and intrapsychic reasons. For instance, one member habitually reports her problems as being largely in the past and currently resolved. She leaves little room for others to comment fruitfully and thus controls the interpersonal interaction and diminishes her own sense of vulnerability. The successful concealment of internal chaos and turmoil and the inability of members to offer her any feedback confirm to her that matters really are in hand. All group members agreed that, as long as a facade of control can be maintained, things have not gotten too bad.

That facade is also an important antidote to the uncertainty that members feel about whether they can will themselves to be different from their alcoholic parents. They see indecision and the acceptance of advice as evidence of lack of control. Intense feelings of depression, loss, and joy are all experienced primarily as a feeling of being out of control and are accompanied by feelings of anxiety, panic, and vulnerability. More important and frightening than the actual emotion is the sense of lack of control.

The other side of the issue of control — feelings of deprivation, depression, loss, and intense dependency needs — are well-disguised and hidden. The intense emphasis on control is a rigid defense to protect against acknowledging the overwhelming threat of that underlying neediness.

The Issue Of Trust

Trust is of profound importance on at least two levels. Members are aware of their distrust of others as long as they closely monitor and control their emotional expressions. At the same time, they are faced with a profound lack of self-trust, as evidenced by continual questioning about the validity of their own feelings and the manipulative quality of the expression of those feelings. They assume that others, like themselves, are controlled by and accept responsibility for fixing bad feelings. They believe a myth of self-control that dictates that feelings are revealed for the specific effect they will have on others. Furthermore, members fear that trusting others is tantamount to granting them increased control. "If I trust you," one member said, "I give a piece of myself to you, and I can't be sure what you'll do with it." Finally, people with intense feelings of anger, sadness, vulnerability, and deprivation can control those emotions by doubting their validity.

Members distrust not only their feelings but the validity of their perceptions. Children who confront parents about their alcoholism are often told that it isn't true, that they see incorrectly or are bad for noticing at all. In the end, the adult children of alcoholics continue to ignore direct experience in favor of the facade for the sake of maintaining an extremely tenuous *status quo*. The wretched nature of th conflict is summed up in one member's feeling that cannot believe that others really are interested in list to her. By openly requesting their attention, she must automatically distrust the sincerity of their response, since her request omnipotently obligates them to listen. The following passage demonstrates the intimate interrelationships between feelings of vulnerability, expressions of emotion, and trust:

> Gradually it became clear that Nancy's vulnerability increased as she revealed emotion to other people, and particularly as she worried that others might see her emotions as phony. This was a potential source of deep hurt for her. Nancy was dealing with a topic that had many, many levels of importance. To begin with, there is the vulnerability that comes simply from the expression of emotion. Along with this is vulnerability that comes from fearing that she might be expressing emotion in a way that was designed to get sympathy. Then finally there is the level of worrying whether others might see her as phony when she is expressing real emotion.

The Issue Of Personal Needs

Members experience the open acknowledgment of personal needs as a source of guilt (by assuming that others are powerless to avoid the imposition), vulnerability (since others will sense their position of increased control and use it arbitrarily), and dependence (a one-down position that is inimical to feeling in control). Members believe that an important means of survival during their childhood was to be dependent only at carefully selected moments: when dependence was demanded or when others were free to attend to their needs. As a consequence, the acknowledgment of needs was uncoupled from internal realities. Children expressed their needs in rhythm with the parent's ability to attend to them or at a moment when reparations must be extracted for past injustices and inattention. from the summary illustrates the issue:

learned to entertain herself and take care of because she felt constantly abandoned and she had always been able to solve her own ause her parents' own needs were so great. In addition, to have needs of her own was an implied criticism of her parents for not meeting them. Jane's dilemma: she needs to make others feel important and needed, as she did for her parents, but at the same time she must not demand or take anything from them.

The Issue Of Responsibility

Members continually overassume responsibility for the feelings and actions of others. This issue likely stems from two main sources: the disowning of responsibility modeled by the alcoholic parent (combined with the tendency of the children to accept what others have disowned) and a more fundamental blurring of boundaries in which children and parents do not feel a separate sense of self, with roles constantly being confused and reversed. The result was a feeling common to all group members that any expression of anger, sadness, or criticism caused an increase of friction within the family, thus driving the alcoholic to drink. It became the child's task to fade into the woodwork whenever necessary in order to avoid being cited as the cause of the alcoholism. At the same time, a unique special relationship developed between the child and the alcoholic parent. The child frequently tried to control the situation by rescuing the alcoholic or by trying to remove the necessity for drinking. The overachieving, model child accomplished the latter by becoming "perfect" or by providing for all the needs of the alcoholic, as a parent does with an infant. In assuming responsibility for the parent's drinking, the child also assumed responsibility for the parent's daily abandonment of him or her. Within the group, members frequently feel an ancient and powerful tug to abort their own and others' expressions of anguish or anger. Each needs to have the others remain in control, and each feels responsible to help combat any deviations from such control.

During the first month of the group, one member's alcoholic father died accidentally. The following passage highlights the special relationship that often exists between a child and an alcoholic parent.

Jane acknowledged the expressions of concern at her father's death and then began explaining her reaction to this loss. She is angry that he left her, yet she wavers between feeling very close to him and needing to be away from him. Overall, she feels he occupied a more central, special role in her life than any other family figure. The anger stems in part from Jane's need to feel that he was really and wholly her father, an older man who would care for her. Now he is gone. A sense of relief comes when she considers that his suffering has ended, but this seems overshadowed by a more powerful sense of hopelessness. Jane always had the hope that she would be able to help him "get well," and that he would eventually recover for her.

The Issue Of Feelings

As noted above, feelings in general are seen to be bad. That view becomes understandable when anger, abandonment, loss, sadness, rejection, and deprivation are the major feelings uncovered by pulling the veil of denial.

Not only is the child denied the intimacy and structure of a normal parent-child relationship, but childhood itself is aborted. In that regard, several members stressed the importance of seeing themselves in the role of a child in the group. It was only when they were identified as children of alcoholics that they could give themselves permission to take. One member, longing to be dependent, wishes openly that she could let go of control. Another wishes that someone could hold her and take care of her for a while. Both are angry at having had to abandon action on those feelings during childhood. Each survived by being less of a child, resorting to a controlled, vigilant existence. Recognition in therapy that the responsibility for that abandonment lies squarely on the parents' shoulders unleashes the vengeful anger of any normal child. Recognition of that abandonment as an adult betrays the fantasy of a special relationship with the alcoholic parent and, in many cases, the nonalcoholic parent as well.

May explained that she agreed to a church wedding "for my mother's sake." With embarrassment, she warned the minister that her mother was likely to drink to excess at the rehearsal dinner. The minister tried to relieve May's anxiety, saying that many of the church members were aware of her mother's drinking problem. May immediately felt a deep sense of betrayal. No one in the church had ever acted on their knowledge of her mother's alcoholism or out of concern for May's having to grow up in an alcoholic family. She then came to feel a new sense of betrayal by her father, who had always pretended to help but had never really confronted the problem. The result, May feels, was that she was left with a pervasive legacy of distrust and an immense feeling of aloneness. May added that these feelings and her childhood methods of coping with them have become restrictive during her adult years.

Finally, control of one's feelings is often used in order to protect others from one's overwhelming out of control and long-suppressed fury.

At the end of the meeting Jane mentioned she wanted to return to one thing that had been noted in the previous summary. She told the group that her emotions were too strong. Her anger and sadness are so great that she feels they would be overwhelming and destructive if released from control. At times it is important for her to sink back into herself in order to keep her feelings from overwhelming her. She asked the group directly to change the subject whenever they see her needing to retreat from her feelings. She says she must control her own tears and emotions because they will be too much for others.

Outcome

Because it is a pilot study, no definitive statements regarding outcome can be made. However, we can report our subjective observations and their implications.

Apart from one college student who terminated after two months because of her school's summer break (agreed on by the group members in advance), adherence to weekly attendance and the nine-month commitment has been nearly total. Two others who terminated expressed satisfaction with recent life and career changes, attributed in part to the therapy. A fourth member terminated feel-

ing stuck, but called six months later to express apprecia-
tion for what she had learned from the group. The remaining members (one original member among them) are
continuing beyond the initial nine-month commitment,
actively entering ever more deeply into therapy.

Discussion

Before discussing our observations, we will look briefly
at the current literature. In our review we find little
research focusing on treatment for the offspring of alcoholics and virtually no research on adults from alcoholic
households (El-Guebaly and Offord, 1977). Jackson (1954)
proposed that alcoholism had disturbing effects on the
personality of family members. Steinglass (1979) docu-
mented that alcoholic families display a wider range of
problem-solving strategies than do schizophrenic, delinquent, or normal families but a more rigid interactional
style. Furthermore, persons within alcoholic families tend
to act more independently during periods of active drinking
but in more rigidly coordinated patterns during dry periods. The effects noted in the children of alcoholics are a
low self-concept (Bosma, 1975); distrust and hiding behind
a defensive facade (Fox, 1962); intense defiance, aggression,
and anxiety (Parnitzke and Prussing, 1966); authority conflicts and unfulfilled dependency needs (Fairchild, 1964).
Seixas (1977) described the child as being robbed of attention, consistent discipline, and a trustworthy environment.
And, in studying 39 children of alcoholics, Fine, Yudin,
Holmes and Heineman (1976) found them to be more
disturbed than the children from a control group in which
a parent suffered from some other psychiatric disorder.
Several of the studies do suggest that effects tend to exert
their strongest influence during adolescence and early
adulthood. We assume that the lack of research reflects, in
part, society's generally ambivalent attitude toward the use
of alcohol. On the one hand, the existence of parental
alcoholism is usually a closely guarded family secret, rarely
acknowledged to anyone outside the immediate family and

often never acknowledged between family members themselves. Thus, in many families, what is most obvious and problematic is also most vehemently denied. On the other hand, alcohol is generally accepted as a legitimate vehicle for social interaction, and anything short of chronic, blatant intoxication is often viewed with amusement. To document serious or potentially serious effects on children growing up in an alcoholic atmosphere is to challenge the too-easy acceptance of its use, to intrude into the privacy of the family, and to open our eyes to unpleasantness.

More extensive clinical studies are needed before our impressions can be more than tentative. Our experience to date does suggest the existence of a recognizable pattern of conflicts carried by the children of alcoholics into their adult lives. Within that pattern of conflicts, issues of control are likely to be paramount. Adult children of alcoholics can be expected to view control issues with particular intensity. Understanding that intensity begins with an examination of family dynamics in an alcoholic household.

In terms of family structure, adult children of alcoholics share a history on several levels. In addition to contact with the alcoholic parent or parents, there is exposure to a family system that was rigid, often chaotic, and frequently rife with pressure to keep the obvious unnoticed. The nonalcoholic parent tends to discourage confrontation of the alcoholic reality while encouraging, by example, the offspring's feelings of responsibility for the alcoholic's success or failure. Members recalled instructions from the nonalcoholic parent to help keep the family peace, lest they pressure the alcoholic parent beyond his or her tolerance and thus precipitate another bout of intoxication. Those instructions result in the offspring's growing up in an atmosphere of arbitrariness and changing limits. Adult children of alcoholics have in common the experience that one day a serious piece of misbehavior was laughed at by a drunken parent, and the next day a normal bit of youthful exuberance was severely chastised by a projecting, guilt-ridden, and perhaps hungover parent. The child's well-being becomes tied to the alcoholic whims of the parent, leading to a constant scanning of the environment for external clues to stave off disaster. The child learns not how to predict the interpersonal consequences of action, since others' reactions are often arbitrary and mysterious, but, instead, how to manage the reactions and behavior of others. That management is best accomplished by learning to control one's own feelings, parceling out their expression to fit the intoxicated parent's particular mood, and dealing with whatever misinterpretation they may encounter. Although alcohol-free families are also capable of engendering hypervigilance and concern for issues of control among the offspring, a unique poignancy seems to exist in the secondary gain that the adult children of alcoholics receive from their sense of control. Primarily, it is a gain in their sense of self-worth, which is greatly enhanced by feelings of having matters in control. That pride in control stems directly from the special relationship with the alcoholic parent so often referred to by group members. Bateson (1971) described the alcoholic personality structure as containing a built-in flaw, identified as the pride that the alcoholic places in self-control. "Pride places the alcoholism outside the self" (Bateson, 1971) and accepts the risk of resisting it. Pride also spurs the alcoholic on in a determined effort to test that self-control; that testing eventually pushes the alcoholic into failure. The alcoholic believes that the problem is one of willpower, and it is precisely that view of the problem that causes it to continue. Intoxication is seen as a weakness, as being out of control, and sobriety is framed as a matter of strength, willpower, and self-control. The child sees control in a similar light. Therefore, to ask the child of an alcoholic to relinquish control is to ask him or her to reject the family norm and myth for attaining self-worth. One expects our adult patients to react with intense anxiety, as was the case among our group members.

Some may question whether parental alcoholism differs from such early stresses as chronic illness and disability. In addition to the ironic and false value placed on control, the ingestion of a substance that alters the apparent personality of the parent is also unique. The child is left to react to the chaos not only within the family structure but also within the actual personality of the adult. The drive of the alcoholic to care less eventually becomes a survival mechanism for the child. Later in life, when purely psychological mechanisms become inadequate to continue suppression of uncontrollable feelings, an extremely high proportion of the adult children of alcoholics resort to the use of alcohol to bolster their efforts to feel normal.

The value of formally labeling the patterns we have described lies in the following areas. (1) The therapist is provided with useful guidelines in the exploration of an individual patient's past. (2) The adult child of an alcoholic seems relatively free to acknowledge the need for psychological help within a framework that externalizes the source of discomfort in an appropriate and perhaps long-overdue manner. (3) The grouping together of persons who have identified themselves as the adult children of alcoholics presents immediate possibilities for bonding and commitment to the group. Many of the advantages of self-help and consciousness-raising groups can be incorporated into a therapeutic setting, primarily through the shared label of being an adult child of an alcoholic.

May then reminded the group that they were all adult children of alcoholics, and suggested they look at what this meant they had in common. From this moment until the end of the session, the meeting took an entirely new tone. Members readily agreed that each has problems in the area of expressing anger, and each has a tendency to project a facade of having themselves "under control." A number of possible explanations for how an alcoholic parent had contributed to these specific problems were discussed and members began sharing their childhood experiences. Jane recalled getting home from school with something to share, but needing to enter the house carefully to assess how safe it was first. Everyone in the group had shared this experience. Tim asked how they as children had been able to express anger at a parent for being drunk. Members laughed bitterly and a flood of anecdotes followed.

Conclusion

Conflicts concerning issues of control, trust, personal needs, responsibility and feelings have been observed in the adult children of alcoholics. Those conflicts stem directly from the coping styles of the alcoholic and the effect of the alcoholism on the family. Group therapy is described as a particularly beneficial therapeutic modality.

References

1. Ablon, J., "Family structure and behavior in alcoholism: A review of the literature," in **The Biology of Alcoholism: IV. Social Aspects of Alcoholism,** (Eds.), B. Kissin and H. Begleiter. New York: Plenum Publishing, 1976.

2. Bateson, G., "The cybernetics of 'self': A theory of alcoholism," in *Psychiatry,* 34:1-18, 1971.

3. Bosma, W., "Alcoholism and teenagers," *Md. State Med. J.,* 24:62-68, 1975.

4. Bowen, M., "Alcoholism as viewed through family systems theory and family psychotherapy," in *Ann. N.Y. Acad. Sci.,* 233:115-122, 1974.

5. Brown, S. and Yalom, I., "Interactional group therapy with alcoholics," in *J. Stud. Alcohol,* 38:426-456, 1977.

6. El-Guebaly, N. and Offord, D.R., "The offspring of alcoholics: A critical review," in *Am. J. Psychiatry,* 134:357-365, 1977.

7. Fairchild, D.M.J., "Teenage children of alcoholic parents," in *Ft. Logan Ment. Health Center,* 2:71-75, 1964.

8. Fine, E., Yudin, L., Holmes, J. and Heineman, S., "Behavioral disorders in children with parental alcoholism," in *Ann. N.Y. Acad. Sci.,* 273:507-517, 1976.

9. Fox, R., "Children in the alcoholic family," in **Problems in Addiction: Alcoholism and Narcotics,** (Ed.), W.C. Bier. New York: Fordham University Press, 1962.

10. Jackson, J.K., "The adjustment of the family to the crisis of alcoholism," in *Q.J. Stud. Alcohol.,* 15:562-686, 1954.

11. Parnitzke, K.H. and Prussing, O., "Children of alcoholic parents," in *Psychol. Abstracts,* 40-647, 1966.

12. Seixas, F., "Children from alcoholic families," in **Alcoholism: Developments, Consequences, and Interventions,** (Eds.) Estes and Heineman, St. Louis: Mosby, 1977.

13. Steinglass, P., "The alcoholic family in the interaction laboratory," in *J. Nerv. Ment. Dis.*, 167:428-436, 1979.

14. ___, Weiner, S. and Mendelson, J., "A systems approach to alcoholism," in *Arch. Gen. Psychiatry*, 24:401-408, 1971.

15. Yalom, I., **The Theory and Practice of Group Psychotherapy.** New York: Basic Books, 1970.

16. ___, "Group psychotherapy and alcoholism," in *Ann. N.Y. Acad. Sci.*, 223:85-103, 1974.

17. ___, Brown, S. and Bloch, S., "The written summary as a group psychotherapy technique," in *Arch. Gen. Psychiatry*, 32:605-613, 1975.

A Developmental Framework For Understanding The Adult Children Of Alcoholics

by *Susan G. Beletsis, Ph.D.*
and
Stephanie Brown, Ph.D.

Introduction

In the last decade the recognition of alcoholism as a family disease has generated much research in the areas of family interaction, the structure and function of the alcoholic family system, and intervention techniques. For the most part these studies have focused on the manner in which the family members act as a part of a system to maintain the drinking, the delineation of the role of the co-alcoholic, and effective methods of intervention which might lead to a new system supporting sobriety and recovery.

Recently there has been an increased focus on the individual members of the alcoholic family, particularly the children. In a critical review of the literature, El-Guebaly and Offord concluded that the offspring of alcoholics were at risk for the more serious psychological illnesses as adults as a consequence of early family environment. This concern for the serious and long-term effects is reflected in the studies of Booz-Allen, Cork and Seixas. It was our concern for the serious repercussions and our belief that a great number of those with problems were not evident, or obvious, and therefore could not enter the mental health system through traditional doors that prompted us to develop a program specifically for the adult children of alcoholics (ACA).

In this paper we will discuss our experiences treating the ACAs at the Stanford Alcohol Clinic during the last four years. Cermak and Brown found in their pilot group for adult children of alcoholics that the offspring tend to experience a recognizable pattern of interpersonal discomfort and intrapsychic conflicts during their adult years which developed in the context of the dysfunctional alcoholic family system. They also found that dynamic interactional group therapy previously found helpful with alcoholic patients, has unique benefits as a therapeutic modality for the adult children of alcoholics.

We continue to find that long-term interactional group therapy provides the necessary potential for bonding and commitment to the group as well as an immediate "family context" in which to explore the past as it is recreated in the present. There are many advantages to the group as a treatment modality, including the presence of the members as a substitute family or support network during a process which is often experienced as difficult and painful. Many see their entry into the group as equal to abandoning their family of origin. Ongoing work at unraveling the past and validating childhood realities keeps these fears of abandonment and loss very much alive.

As awareness of the group therapy for ACAs has grown, we have added groups and offered individual psychotherapy concurrently for many of these individuals. There are presently two women's groups and two male-female groups, a mix that reflects the significantly greater number of women than men seeking help. It is not yet clear to us whether this is the result of a general tendency for women to utilize mental health services more than men, or whether certain roles with long-term consequences are more often given to a female child in the alcoholic family.

We will expand the descriptive background provided by our patients and elaborate some of the clinical concepts presented in the original study, particularly as they relate to inadequately achieved developmental tasks within the context of the dysfunctional alcoholic family system. The theoretical material reported in this paper stems from our work with both men and women, while the clinical material comes entirely from women. It is the main purpose of this paper to integrate our clinical theories and observations with a developmental model. We are speaking mainly about women, yet we are in no way ready to postulate differences between these two groups.

Family Environment

It is clear from our adult children of alcoholics that not every child is affected by the alcoholic parent in the same way. Psychological, social and interactional factors give rise to a variety of adaptations. In addition, the dynamics of the family environment differ depending on such variables as whether one or both parents are alcoholic; the children's ages when the alcoholism becomes unmanageable; economic stability; and, the availability and use of external support systems.

Despite these differences, our patients reveal many commonalities and identifiable patterns of adaptation to the alcoholism. We are increasing our knowledge of the difficulties in mastering developmental tasks by examining their consensually validated memories of experiences and our own assessment of the consequences of such a childhood environment. With this understanding we are in a position to offer sensitive and informed therapeutic treatment to adult children of alcoholics as well as improving our strategies for early intervention with the estimated 15 to 18 million children presently living with an alcoholic parent.

We begin our exploration by examining the evidence in alcoholic families. In general, the family atmosphere is characterized by chaos and unpredictability. There is an inconsistency of behavioral expectations and limits, physical and emotional care and responsiveness to communication and interactions. In most alcoholic families there is a major secret — the alcoholism — and this secret is the central focus around which the family becomes organized. The primary defense used to maintain this secret is denial, although the level of denial varies considerably. In some families the alcoholism is never acknowledged, in others it may be recognized, while the impact and the seriousness are denied or explained away as the result of other problems. Most of our group members come from families where the alcoholism has never been acknowledged by *all* family members as the central problem.

Because what is most visible and problematic, the alcoholism, is most vehemently denied, children are early caught up in the difficult task of joining in the denial process, or facing continuous threats to their own perceptions of reality. As all available energy goes into coping with the reality and maintaining the denial, the focus shifts, for the non-alcoholic spouse as well as the children, to "making the alcoholic well" or to simply surviving in spite of what is really happening. A group member revealed the paralyzing strength of the denial as well as the perpetual double bind, in telling why she had never sought help from a school counselor or gone to Alateen:

> In our family there were two very clear rules: The first was that there is nothing wrong here, and the second was, don't tell anyone.*

Under these circumstances the alcoholic family becomes increasingly isolated and defensive. There is often a great deal of shame and fear, necessitating withdrawal from friends, community, church and health services. As the alcoholism progresses there may be many job changes and frequent moves furthering the sense of isolation and resulting in increased intra-family tension. The alcoholic, often presented as the victim of external circumstances, actually has enormous control over the family. His or her behavior sets the rules directly or indirectly that must be followed by family members regardless of how arbitrary or inconsistent they may seem.

In this atmosphere, childhood is short or nonexistent. The child learns to "manage" the actions of others, always attempting to ward off disaster. Children learn what is expected in certain situations, responding often to nonverbal clues in a constantly unpredictable climate. The child learns to parcel out feelings so as to avoid upsetting the alcoholic or being held responsible for precipitating a drinking bout. Thus the child's feelings, needs and behavior are dictated by the state of the alcoholic at any given and unpredictable time in the drinking cycle. All members of the family struggle to find ways of controlling a situation which cannot be controlled.

The emphasis on denial in the alcoholic family and the reality of the inconsistency and unpredictability lead to a predominance of defensive coping stategies. There is a

---

*All quotes and case material in this article are taken from the edited summaries of group meetings.

constant threat that the family secret may be discovered or that some disaster resulting from the alcoholism will occur within the family. As a result, it is very difficult to accurately assess personal needs and to identify and act on feelings. For the child, the defensive posture is necessary to survival and becomes all-encompassing.

Keeping this general overview of the alcoholic family system in mind, we will now move to a more specific description of the developmental difficulties for the child growing up in such a family. Again, it is important to note that in seeking patterns of adaptations and similarities in dysfunctional development, we do not in any way deny the infinite variety of individual differences and unique experiences of each child and family. Rather, we seek to describe, within a developmental framework, those common experiences which increase understanding of the etiology of the serious and long-term problems presented by those adult children of alcoholics who come for help at the alcohol clinic.

Stages Of Development

Basic Trust

Erikson and Mahler have both postulated detailed theoretical frameworks from which to view psychosocial development. Each conceives of certain basic tasks, and the resolution of conflict or crisis, necessary at stage specific times during the emotional development in childhood.

For the very young child, the development of trust is crucial. During the first year of life the child is completely dependent on the accurate responsiveness of the mother to meet basic physical and emotional needs. While the development of trust is not an achievement, but rather an ongoing process, basic trust, developed in the context of an adequate symbiotic relationship with the mother, is the necessary cornerstone for a healthy attitude toward self and other in interpersonal relationships.

In a family where the mother is an alcoholic, the mother-infant relationship will be impaired, and perhaps profoundly. The mother's primary emotional involvement is with alcohol and the child's needs are secondary at best. At times the mother does not respond at all to the child's cries and a feeding may be missed or a child left wet and cold for hours. Or the mother may be drunk and tend to the child ineptly, offering unwanted or scalding bottles, holding the child in an uncomfortable way or inadvertently injuring the child. At other times the mother may be hung over, sick with withdrawal symptoms, depressed and guilty, or resentful at having to care for a dependent infant. In either case, appropriate physical care, as well as emotional nourishment, is absent from the interaction.

If the father is the alcoholic, the mother may be preoccupied with problems in the relationship and concern about the alcoholism. Her energy may well be directed towards parenting her husband and coping with the fear and despair. The resulting tension and confusion often results in the psychological abandonment of the child, or in inadequate and inconsistent caretaking. Alternately, the mother may turn to the child as a source of comfort, a replacement for the emotional contact which has been lost, a solution to the unresolvable problem of alcoholism.

If the alcoholic mother is incapable of adequately mothering, whether because of her own alcoholism or preoccupation with an alcoholic spouse, the infant and young child learn to expect inconsistency, inadequate care and general disorganization. As with institutionalized infants, it is likely that the children of alcoholics begin very early to adapt their most basic needs to the random availability of care. It is in this early pattern of interactions that the ability to trust the environment is undermined, causing disturbances which affect all later stages of development.

With the loss of input and responsiveness from the mother at this developmental stage, there is a loss of the mutual regulation process which results in an increase in the child's sense of confidence. It is only through this reciprocal process that confidence and trust in the self develop. The impairment, a sense of basic mistrust and the failure to develop confidence, is expressed in the tendency to deny or adapt needs, the tendency of the child to withdraw, and the conversion of the effort to communicate with and control the environment, into a precocious conscience and over-control of self.

Trust and confidence in self-worth can be betrayed by consistent parental neglect at any stage in the child's development. In the alcoholic family it is likely that it will be betrayed over and over again as the obsession with alcohol increases. However, it is the failure to develop basic trust in the early months of life which is the precursor of the more severe problems with interpersonal relationships, inability to tolerate intimacy, and confusion over the locus of control. In addition, failure at this stage of development results in the unsuccessful differentiation of self from mother. Fueled by unmet needs, the child of an alcoholic remains focused on the parent and cannot experience the appropriate awareness of self as a distinct person. In fact, before any awareness of alcoholism could possibly be present, the child's actions and feelings are controlled to some degree by the presence of alcohol.

Autonomy And Self-control

The ability to move into the second stage of development comprising the many tasks of developing autonomy and self-control is, in great part, dependent on a firmly developed sense of trust in self and other. This is necessary so that the child's survival will not be threatened by the struggle for control of body functions, feelings and all issues of "holding on" and "letting go," closeness and distance. For the child of an alcoholic, already attuned to the parents' needs, to unpredictable responses and inconsistent physical treatment, the developmental tasks at this stage are almost impossible.

In the alcoholic family the parents' ability to provide fair and consistent discipline and flexible and loving external control which is supportive of the child's growing need for autonomy is severely impaired. The alcoholic is struggling daily with issues of impulse control, the non-alcoholic parent struggling to control the alcoholic. For the child who is still trying to differentiate self from the parent it is a time of great confusion. Even at this early age, the pattern may develop of a child desperately eager to please, who develops a compulsive need to do everything correctly. But with an alcoholic parent, what is correct or pleasing in a drunk period may elicit anger, shaming or punishment in a sober period. Impatience, guilt or illness from a hangover all influence the response of the parent far more than the child's behavior does. In this inconsistent setting the child is most likely to develop feelings of shame and doubt, and over-manipulate herself regardless of the damage to autonomy and self-esteem.

It is in this period when the fundamental sense of responsibility for others develops. The child who has unsuccessfully differentiated, has not developed the ego boundaries necessary to discriminate the source of the feelings, who is responsible for whom, nor to risk testing out and defining limits and boundaries. Adult children of alcoholics frequently remember early (second to fourth year) commands which fostered this sense of responsibility: "Don't cry, you will upset your father" (precipitate a drinking bout).

In later childhood this burden of responsibility grows even stronger and at the same time more confusing. Children of alcoholics often do take on many real, though inappropriate, responsibilities within the family. However, they are unable to differentiate the real responsibilities from the perceived responsibility to control or affect the parent's drinking. It is that responsibility which becomes an overwhelming burden. In addition, there is a sense of importance and even omnipotence in their belief that they can do something to help or control the parent, while their experience is one of continuous failure and helplessness. The consequence is an increase in feeling responsible and unrealistic self-demands.

The failure to develop autonomy and to begin the process of separation and individuation leaves these children emotionally locked into a family system which is both increasingly dysfunctional and unresolvable.

Initiative And Mastery

With the adequate development of a differentiated self and an increase in autonomy, the child is able to move increasingly further away from the parent, secure in the knowledge that return for support and comfort is always possible. This process is again, a mutual regulation of the child's growing need for independence and separation and the parents' tolerance as well as pleasure in this growth. In the alcoholic family, the child who is already vulnerable because of the incompleted earlier stages of development is not able to negotiate this increasing separation successfully. The parents preoccupied with alcohol may seize this opportunity to withdraw from parenting, suddenly expecting a level of continuous self-sufficiency which is unreasonable and anxiety-provoking for the child. Rather than a smooth transition, the child is precipitously pushed into early ego development, and insecure independence. Alternatively, a mother may cling to the child in order to alleviate her own sense of loss and isolation or out of guilt, depriving the child of increasing confidence through greater and greater separation.

By the time the child in an alcoholic family reaches school age, the confidence in self-control and the pleasure of increased initiative may already be distorted by feelings of anxiety and inferiority. The child's needs and behavior are increasingly dictated by the state of the alcoholic as well as the non-alcoholic's level of involvement. Defensively, control becomes increasingly important as the child attempts to "manage" the actions and responses of others. The child has begun to "learn the system" of the family.

Many adult children of alcoholics report feeling more competent at six than they do as adults. The tasks taken on by children in alcoholic families seem astonishing: collecting bills, tending younger siblings, buying groceries, putting out cigarettes, and emptying liquor bottles, just to name a few. It is competence driven by necessity and anxiety. The non-alcoholic parent may have to work, often leaving the children with responsibility for themselves as well as for the drinking parent.

It is not surprising that the outward appearance of this child, school performance, responsibility and apparent maturity, is very often the result of the development of a "false self," different from the subjective experience of doubt, inadequacy, and an overwhelming feeling of responsibility. The child becomes the family's messenger to the outside world demonstrating that the family is all right. The child has become an extension of the parents' needs, a part of the system in denying the alcoholism.

A stable family environment during this stage of development allows the child to invest energy in intellectual and social development. While the child of an alcoholic may be an excellent student, the sense of responsibility and the drive for perfection, as well as the internal pressure to perform, often increase anxiety and escalate unrealistic expectations. School may become the one predictable arena where children from alcoholic families feel they can achieve some control, although they often experience the feeling that no matter how well they do, it isn't enough.

Because the family environment is so unpredictable and chaotic it is difficult for children to develop and maintain friendships. Embarrassment and shame prevent them from bringing friends to the house and the curiosity of friends and their parents is a continuous threat to the secrecy that protects the alcoholic parent. The important social skills and sense of comfort with peers, necessary to this developmental stage, cannot develop in a context where the child's primary preoccupation is bound up in the survival of the family.

The emphasis on denial as a major defense in the family has a powerful effect on the child. Perceptions are often contradicted by the parents' statements about what they see. The most obvious problem is not labeled, and often not acknowledged. Children may hear a mother blaming her husband's absence from work on the illness of a child, when the child knows this to be untrue. Children become unwilling to develop initiative or demonstrate their mastery when they may be held responsible for events that are outside their control. In this setting there is a constant distortion of reality. To maintain the family homeostasis the children must begin to deny their own reality and accept the distorted reasoning presented by the parents. Even within the family there may be a shifting reality, changing from day to day, or drunk to sober, that the child must adapt to.

Children of alcoholics experience fear and anger, depression and helplessness, and often, despair. Yet they are not permitted to express their own feelings nor act on their needs. Increasingly, they deny their own perceptions and feelings, questioning everything but the alcoholic reality. The very mechanisms which allow for survival — denial, withdrawal, lack of trust and secrecy — cut the child off from learning and demonstrating mastery.

Identification

Throughout developmental stages children make a variety of identifications, sometimes with one parent, then the other, occasionally with an older sibling or relative. The major task of adolescence is an integration of these transitional identifications into an integrated sense of ego identity. The accrued experiences of earlier stages — a trust in the interpersonal environment and self, comfort with a solid feeling of autonomy and independence, and mastery of an appropriate level of intellectual and social skills — have a profound effect on the self-esteem and sense of continuity required for this identification process.

The child of an alcoholic is in a double bind. Coping strategies which depend on not trusting others, denial of perceptions of reality, and the assumption of responsibility for "managing" the actions and well-being of others leave little time for self-exploration and psychological growth. In fact the driving need to deny feelings and needs is a denial of self, and avoidance of having an independent identity. The child of an alcoholic cannot afford to give up the confused role of a child in this dysfunctional system, a re-actor rather than an actor moving toward adulthood.

There may already exist a very strong bond with the alcoholic parent. They both share an experience of help-lessness and failure. The non-alcoholic parent may be seen as critical, depressed, the cause of the drinking, or with-drawn and unavailable as a parent and model. Sometimes the anger and contempt for the alcoholic is recognized and the identification is with the non-alcoholic spouse as a victim. Evidence from the adult children of alcoholics sug-gests that there is usually a primary identification, often unconscious, with the alcoholic — with someone who is out of control.

Whether one or both parents are alcoholic, the magni-tude of the problem and the obsession with the alcohol make it likely that neither parent has been available as an appropriate model throughout childhood. The role rever-sals which have taken place since early childhood leave the child defended against being a dependent child, and de-fended against being an adult parent to the out-of-control alcoholic. The resolution may be an adolescent identity as a "pseudo-adult," feeling helpless and frightened, appearing overly mature and capable, striving for control.

The variety of adaptations at adolescence is enormous. The child may act on the identification with the alcoholic, becoming delinquent and abusing drugs and alcohol. In families where both parents were alcoholic, many adult children report feeling an internal pressure to "join the family," truly belonging by accepting the alcoholism and becoming dependent on alcohol themselves. Many respond to the chaos and confusion they have observed by with-drawing from same and opposite sex peer relationships. Thus, they further isolate themselves from the outside world and from an appropriate investment in long-term relationships which might threaten the primary involve-ment with the family.

Some children leave home early or rush into marriage, often choosing a dependent mate or an alcoholic. In this way they consciously or unconsciously find their way back into a situation that is, at least, familiar and in which they know how to play the role required. If both parents are alcoholics, children may not have had an opportunity to observe a relationship that does not include alcohol. They learn that alcohol is a part of the expression of love, sorrow, joy, anger, frustration and rage. Alcohol as a means of coping with life is seen as normal and it is difficult to imagine a relationship without it.

It is most likely that the child of an alcoholic fails to develop an ego identity based on an integration of capabilities, a confidence in the ability to maintain an inner sense of self-esteem and continuity, and a sense of reality about one's meaning for others. The child whose development has taken place in the context of an alcoholic family is more likely to move through adolescence encumbered by an assumed role, an identity forced on him or her by circumstances beyond control. The result of this identity diffusion and the assumption of a false self, is a growing discord between the facade (how others see me) and the internal experience (how I see myself).

The accumulated problems of earlier developmental failures such as a lack of trust in others and loss of confidence in self, difficulties in differentiation and boundaries, fear of autonomy and the lack of a sense of initiative and mastery have a powerful impact in late adolescence, as the child prepares for the final task of adolescence, leaving the family.

Separation

Many adult children of alcoholics report that whether or not they left home physically at the end of adolescence, they have never been able to separate emotionally. Even from a distance they remain an integral part of the chaos, feeling the family emergencies and the responsibility for caretaking decisions about the alcoholic parent. Often they feel guilty about leaving younger siblings behind in an environment they know to be damaging. Many have left college or marriage and gone back home to "try to fix things" one more time.

The sense of identity and direction as well as the focus on reasonable goals, and a desire to be involved with others and broaden social and intellectual experiences motivates the child with an adequate developmental history to make this move into the outside world. Appropriate earlier experiences of individuation and temporary separations which increased confidence, provide a foundation for the belief that this separation will be a good experience. For the child of an alcoholic, the separation at the end of adolescence is experienced more as abandoning, or being abandoned by, the family. There is anxiety over the ability to survive outside the family, guilt about the family's ability to survive without the child.

Those who leave home to go to school, to work, or to marry immediately find themselves in trouble. Their expectations for themselves are very high. Doing all right means keeping things under control. Keeping things under control often means doing them perfectly, satisfying the boss completely, or having interpersonal relationships in which feelings are hidden and all goes smoothly. Adult children of alcoholics often take on, or experience, an enormous amount of responsibility in all areas of their lives. They have trouble sharing responsibility, feeling this as a loss of control. No matter how well they do, it is never quite enough.

Whether far from home or still near, they often experience themselves as lonely and isolated. Relationships are fraught with difficulty; trust and intimacy are avoided. There is often little prior experience in early adolescence with close peer relationships, and the long experience of denying feelings and needs does not permit reaching out for support or help. Concern for and involvement with the family leaves little attention for the development of new ties and a social network. Many report being extremely depressed, feeling life meaningless, and experiencing continuous feelings of inadequacy and failure. It is tempting to return home where they can experience a definite place in the family system, a feeling of self-worth.

The youngest members of our ACA groups are in their early twenties, struggling with problems of this first separation from family. They are more likely than older members to be actively dealing with their family of origin. They report great difficulty in concentrating on their own goals, are often involved in dysfunctional relationships and have an inordinate need to be in control. Some work at jobs considerably below their potential, while others start at the "top" and experience anxiety at the responsibilities of their precocious career development. Many express feelings of emptiness and feel they have fooled everyone into thinking they are adequate.

They share in common with older group members unresolved emotional bonds with their families, fear and denial of feelings, poor communication skills, role confusion and problems of identification. They are all concerned to one degree or another with alcohol in their own lives, many fearing their own inevitable alcoholism up ahead or in the present. They also share defenses and coping strategies learned in the context of an alcoholic family, an inheritance they must give up in order to survive without becoming dependent on alcohol.

For most adult children of alcoholics, there is little or no awareness of the cumulative effects of their childhood experiences in the alcoholic family. The varied defenses which protected the alcoholic parent work to allow the ACAs to appear, as they did in childhood, adequate or successful. It is often an awareness of the incongruence between how they present themselves and how they actually experience themselves internally, along with a growing fear of becoming alcoholic, that precipitates the first step toward help. The decision to join the group also represents an unconscious decision to give up these maladaptive defenses.

The decision to enter therapy or join a group often represents the first break in the denial system of the individual. For some it is the denial of the parent's alcoholism that has given way. For others, it is denial of their helplessness and sense of failure which must be given up. They join the group with the idea of getting the answer to their life-long problem — how do you help the alcoholic? With this entry they can acknowledge the alcoholism without stepping outside their role. It is a way to get help without abandoning the parent.

It is remarkable that these individuals make the decision to join a group. The conscious wish to separate emotionally from their families and to change themselves conflicts with a deep fear and reluctance, which is a continuing theme in the group. One woman described it this way:

> I feel like I'm involved in a minuet, with intricate and specific dance steps. If I want to step out or do a different step, the whole family is threatened, and I will never get back in.

Members want help out of their families, and at the same time they want to stay in. Since their only sense of self-worth has come from what they have done for the family, the unconscious decision to begin the separation process and to begin relinquishing responsibility for the alcoholic activates intense anxiety and can be experienced not only as a major loss, but a loss of control and a loss of meaning in their lives as well.

The label "adult children of alcoholics" is extremely important. It creates an immediate basis for peer identification and bonding, and provides legitimacy for treatment. One major defense of these individuals has been a strong belief in their ability to control themselves and others and their automatic assumption of responsibility for others. As such, they have never identified themselves as having problems or needing any help. They tend to rely on themselves, attempt to meet all their own needs, and have great difficulty seeing themselves as the "identified patient," the one who needs help. To become an ACA is to assume a new identity, and along with it a legitimate right to treatment.

In describing the major recurrent issues and interactions which become therapeutic issues and are worked through in the group, we will illustrate how closely this clinical material expresses the profound consequences of the developmental experience in an alcoholic family. The clinical examples are taken from the group summaries which are mailed to all members immediately after each group meeting.

Once in the group, individuals recognize that they must begin to make "public" their experiences in their alcoholic families and they must learn to validate their perceptions, so long distorted and invalidated. The group environment permits this process of validation, and it does so by intensifying and re-creating the environment of the family of origin. However, this process is not without conflict and anxiety, for in this "re-created family" they must struggle constantly with the many-faceted issues of control, and their great fear of trusting others to hear, to care, to respond appropriately and to be there consistently.

The inability to trust in the group as a whole, or any single member, reflects the early experience in the child's relationships in the family. It is safer to remain in control, not reveal pain or needs, as a defense against the expected unpredictable, insensitive, or destructive response. Trusting others is equal to giving them control:

> If I trust you, it is like giving a piece of myself to you. And I don't know what you will do with it.

Absences in the group have a major impact on the group process, as members struggle to build trust in the group and allow themselves increased involvement and commitment. One member expressed this fear, as well as her own separation anxiety, when she returned from vacation and said poignantly:

> I had the fantasy that when I came back to the group no one would be here.

The other side of this mistrust is clearly evident in group members' inability to trust themselves. They fear that their own responses will overwhelm the other person, and have great difficulty knowing whether to trust their own perceptions and feelings about the interactions in the group. Control is maintained in the interaction by doubting the validity of their feelings, or by silence which has a powerful effect on others in the group. One woman stated:

My silence and depression is just like my father's alcoholism, it controls everyone around me.

Given this lack of trust of self as well as others, the resolution is often to be found in caring for and taking responsibility for others. The reasoning behind this can be expressed, perhaps exactly as the child constructed it. "I will be quiet, I will be good. I will deny or ignore my feelings and try to care for this other person in the hope that if I am successful, then the other person will intuit my needs and take care of them." The chronic frustration and helplessness that results from this pattern of behavior often leads to depression and hopelessness, as the intense anger, a more natural response, is too overwhelming and would be experienced as out of control.

The powerful need for control over the environment and in relationships reflects the great difficulty children of alcoholics have in differentiating from their parents and in developing a comfortable level of autonomy. Their own behavior and need for independent action is seen, first by the parent, and now by themselves as a terrible threat to any feeling of security. Self-responsibility and self-control are eroded by their feeling responsible for others, and the failure to control others forces them back into more self-limitations and a feeling of being controlled.

Within the group, members often feel controlled by another's response. Silence indicates criticism or disinterest. Too much support or too many solutions to an upsetting problem may be interpreted as a command to get things back under control. Interruptions and distracting comments often mask the automatic attempt to protect a member from losing control. Coming late to sessions, or missing a session is often related to problems with autonomy and control, a testing of the response from other members. Often, when one member becomes emotional in describing a problem in her life, another will feel manipulated by such an expression of feelings and act quickly to control or limit them.

Jean tends to be very emotional in the group as she tries to express her frustration with another member. As she starts to cry, a third member, Linda, looks away with a bored and somewhat disgusted look. Jean immediately stops crying and becomes concerned with what Linda is feeling, aborting her own work and responding to Linda's acknowledged anxiety "when things get out of control."

These two members often repeat this interaction, until they begin to see that Linda invariably reacts as a frightened and controlling child (or non-alcoholic parent) to what she experiences as Jean's loss of control (alcoholic) and unresolvable problems.

Group members spend much time exploring the dynamics of their relationships outside the group as well as with each other. For most of them, difficulty with intimacy sparked by the lack of trust, and compounded by their lack of autonomy and ego boundaries, makes interpersonal relationships threatening and dissatisfying. During those years when learning intellectual and social skills increases comfort with peers and self-esteem, the children of alcoholics were mastering complex and shifting roles and relationships in a dysfunctional family system. Communication skills developed in a context which demanded denial and distortion of their perceptions of reality. In the group, members attempt to work through and improve these relationships, tentatively building up trust, exploring their anxiety about their own needs and feelings, and correcting and validating their perceptions of themselves and others. One woman, early in the group, described this process:

I feel like this is a chance to discover a real me, and learn how to be in a real world. There must be a way to be that won't be annihilated by every word of criticism.

In work, as well as in relationships, adequacy of functioning is often determined by all-or-none assessment. Either I am doing it perfectly or I am a complete failure. These evaluations are usually determined by assumptions about what other people will think. The adult child of an alcoholic is determined to succeed, to master, to control. It is life-threatening not to. But this intense need developed in the struggle with the alcoholic, where success was measured by controlling the parent's drinking, which was out of control.

Group members explore, over and over again, the intricacies of their relationships with each other as trust and commitment move the group to a different level of intimacy. They must work out the nature of appropriate responsibility to each other, increase tolerance for differences and autonomy, and recognize their inability to control others. In this way they begin to develop boundaries which protect them from unreasonable demands. They build trust in themselves that they do not have the power to overwhelm and become a destructive force to someone else. It is a long and often painful process.

Perhaps the most painful part of the process is understanding and coping with their identification with both parents. Children of alcoholics cannot withdraw far enough within the family to avoid a strong identification with one parent. Often they make a paradoxical and incongruent identification with both, which remains in adulthood, with one side split off and out of awareness. Behind the critical-demanding or depressed-victim identification with the non-alcoholic parent is often a great fear of losing control, of becoming the alcoholic. In those who experience themselves consciously as being more disorganized, more helpless and dependent, there is often a strong internal identification with the critical-demanding parent who can never be appeased.

In a women's group where members often shift back and forth, unwittingly relating to each other in one or both of these roles, the topic of their own alcohol use is approached tentatively and with caution. While the identifications with both parents have many implications on many different levels, it is this fear of inevitably losing control and becoming an alcoholic that is most difficult to deal with. After months in the group, Joan spoke of it this way:

I feel shabby most of the time, like my mother. I have such high expectations and feel critical of myself most of the time. When I'm disappointed and depressed I know why my mother drank all the time.

Another member, her own fear and anxiety triggered by this comment, returned to this statement several times during the meeting, attempting to get her to change or withdraw her empathic identification.

Issues of separation are dealt with in the group from the very first meeting until termination. For adult children of alcoholics, to be different is to risk rejection and separation. To be close and depend on the group touches anxiety about loss. Leaving a meeting concerned about an upset member or unresolved problems is often a means of maintaining the connection until the group meets again. One member, thinking about leaving the group for a variety of reasons, spoke of her feelings about leaving for several meetings without making the decision to leave definite. Her exploration of this topic raised such anxiety and anger in another member that she finally commented in an angry outburst:

You are just like my mother! Every month she would get fed up with my father's drinking and she packed a suitcase and put it by the door. She told us kids she was leaving but my father would cry and plead with her and she always unpacked her bag and stayed. I never got over being terrified when she packed her bag.

Appropriate separation from the group tests all the therapeutic work done by group members, in terms of how stable the present identification of self is, how well the individual is able to limit the demands of others and express her own needs and feelings, what changes have been made creating the potential for mature relationships with others permitting trust and intimacy, and the ability to define the limits of responsibility for and control of others. Not all members stay in the group long enough to complete this work, but many do. Others leave with a foundation built on the validation of their experience, and the corrective experience that occurs in the group which permits later work on many of these issues.

The process of recovery for the adult children of alcoholics involves a revision of the past. The facts of a childhood spent in a family with an alcoholic parent do not change. The memories remain detailed and vivid. However, the meaning attributed by the child to these events, gives way to a cognitive restructuring. Based on the validation of experience in a reparative therapeutic setting, this restructuring alters the belief system which mandated certain defenses as necessary to survival and allows for the development of more appropriate and adaptive defenses.

The identification as a child in this group experience permits regression to earlier modes of experiencing and reacting, as well as the chance to move through earlier developmental stages in a new and constructive context. The identification as a child contains within it the understanding that psychological growth will occur, each phase of the group process building on the successful working through and mastery of the issues in the preceding phase.

This process reflects the original developmental sequence, although the sequence is not linear in the group work. Denial must give way in order to be a member. Basic trust develops slowly against tremendous resistance. Members must be continuously testing their perceptions of reality, learning to set limits, and increasing their autonomy. As an adult identification develops, a sense of independence and strength permits separation from the group.

References

1. Ablon, J., "The significance of cultural patterning for the alcoholic family," in *Family Process*, 19:127-144, 1980.
2. Booz-Allen and Hamilton, "Final report on the needs and resources for children of alcoholic parents," NIAAA, Rockville, Md., 1974.
3. Bowen, M., "Alcoholism as viewed through family systems theory and family psychotherapy," in *Ann. N.Y. Academy of Science*, 233:115-122, 1974.

4. Brown, S. and Yalom, I.D., "Interactional group therapy with alcoholics," in *Journal of Studies on Alcohol*, 38:426-456, 1977.

5. Cermak, T. and Brown, S., "Interactional group therapy with adult children of alcoholics," *International Journal of Group Psychotherapy*, Vol. 32, 375-389, 1982."

6. Cork, R.M., **The Forgotten Children.** Toronto: Paper Jacks, 1969.

7. El-Guebaly, N. and Offord, D., "The offspring of alcoholics: A critical review," in *Journal of Psychiatry*, 134:357-365, 1977.

8. Erikson, E.H., "Identity and the life cycle," Monograph Vol. 1, No. 1. New York: International University Press, 1959.

9. _____, **Childhood And Society,** New York: W.W. Norton, 1963.

10. Estes, N.J. and Heinemann, M.E., (Eds.), **Alcoholism: Development, Consequences And Interventions.** St. Louis: C.V. Mosby, 1977.

11. Fox, R., "The effects of alcoholism on children," New York: National Council on Alcoholism pamphlet, 1972.

12. Mahler, M.S., Pine, F. and Bergman, A., **The Psychological Birth Of The Human Infant.** Basic Books, 1975.

13. Seixas, J., "Children from alcoholic families," in Estes, N.J. and Heinemann, M.E., (Eds.), **Alcoholism: Development, Consequences And Interventions.** St. Louis: C.V. Mosby, 1977.

14. Steinglass, P., "The alcoholic family in the interaction laboratory," in *Journal on Nervous and Mental Disease*, 167:428-436, 1979.

15. Strachan, J.G., **Alcoholism: Treatable Illness.** Vancouver, B.C.: Mitchell Press, 1968.

16. Wilson, C., and Orford, J., "Children of alcoholics: Report of a preliminary study and comments on the literature," in *Journal of Studies on Alcoholism*, 19:121-142, 1978.

17. Yalom, I.D., **The Theory and Practice of Group Psychotherapy.** New York: Basic Books, 1970.

18. _____, Brown, S. and Bloch, S., "The written summary as a group psychotherapy technique," in *Archives of General Psychiatry*, 32:605-613,1975.

The Development Of Family Transference In Groups For The Adult Children Of Alcoholics

by Stephanie Brown, Ph.D.
and
Susan G. Beletsis, Ph.D.

Introduction

For nearly four years, we have been building at the Stanford Alcohol Clinic a pioneer program for adults who identify themselves as the adult children of alcoholics (ACA). We have reported on the origin of our work and our observations of a pilot group in an initial paper (Cermak and Brown, 1981) and more recently have applied a developmental framework to our understanding of the child's experience in an alcoholic home (Beletsis and Brown, 1981). We continue to be impressed with the enormous impact and long-range consequences of growing up in an alcoholic family. Our program has grown from one long-term therapy group to four, with a long waiting list. Many ACAs are in individual therapy as well as the group, or while waiting to join the group.

Over the course of our work, we have kept detailed process records of all group meetings (names are fictitious in this paper) which are mailed to group members as well (Yalom, Brown, and Bloch, 1975). It is through these summaries that we can reconstruct in careful detail the main clinical issues which arise over time, particularly the evolution of family transference among the members. (Direct quotations from summaries are indented.) By family transference is meant the tendency to view the group as the family of origin and to behave in the group as one once did in that first family. Although now described in many other places in terms of family roles and environment (Black, 1981; Wegscheider, 1981; El-Guebaly and Offord, 1977, 1979), we have come to recognize that the issue of alcoholism in the family of origin is of critical ongoing dynamic importance to the adult children of alcoholics.

In this paper, we will demonstrate the continuing significance and varied meanings of alcohol in the family in terms of real-life concerns as well as the development of a family transference within the group. Any attempt to understand and interpret the transference phenomena which develop in an ACA group requires a detailed understanding of the subjective experience as well as the major interpersonal issues in the alcoholic family which are the sources of this family transference.

The Decision To Join

The decision to join the group is the first link in the development of an active transference although it also represents a conscious decision to break a lifetime pattern of denial and to open a closed and often secret family history. Members recognize intuitively that by joining, they will awaken and intensify a bond to their families in the long-term interest of achieving a physical and emotional separation, not accomplished at the appropriate time in their development.

The decision to join represents a commitment to "make real the past," to say what really happened and thereby let go of a life-long major family secret: a secret that still binds many to their families. But there is an enormous threat in doing so. Much important work in therapy takes place before actually beginning the group in the agonizing process of first calling oneself the child of an alcoholic, and then deciding to join the group to make public that truth.

Acceptance of the label "ACA" often brings forth a flood of forgotten, painful memories. Members frequently equate a decision to join the group with betrayal and abandonment of their families. The label is also felt as an aggressive act: one which will surely result in the rejection of them by their parents. To break denial, to accept a label and to make it public is to orphan oneself.

Mary Ann was extremely self-conscious in the early weeks of the group. She finally acknowledged that she was terribly afraid of being seen attending a group for the children of alcoholics. It was OK for her to be in individual therapy, but she could not accept what she was saying about her mother by belonging to this group. An only child of a single parent, she was always terrified of losing her mother. This move seemed to guarantee it.

Why then would individuals decide to join? The fears of loss and abandonment are countered by a greater fear: what will happen to them if they don't do something? All members have arrived at the decision because of serious problems in their own lives and a recognition that their present difficulties are tied to the past. In their initial interviews and the early weeks of the group, members spell out the connection of their present to the past, underlining the central theme of alcohol.

Many state directly that they want to break their identification with the alcoholic. Many believe that they are already alcoholic and if they do not intervene on their own behalf, they will be powerless to prevent the inevitable — becoming actively alcoholic like their parents.

In a new group of six members, one identified herself as a recovering alcoholic and four identified concern about their own drinking as a major reason for joining the group. The sixth was certain she would be alcoholic if she did not exert careful control. She was tired of the vigilance required to make sure she doesn't drink alcoholically. For this member and many others who identify themselves as nonalcoholic, life is a struggle not to become like the drinking parent(s).

The recovering alcoholic was worried about the reaction of other members to her, thinking they would transfer their feelings about their parents to her. In fact, in the beginning, they envied her instead, because she had made the decision that she was alcoholic and had stopped drinking. This agonizing process, or continuing indecision, lay ahead for the others and they dreaded it.

These individuals recognized that they are overinvolved and overidentified with their alcoholic families. Many still feel responsible for the welfare of their parents and siblings and many, in fact, are actively involved in the care and protection of those families.

A significant number of our ACAs have detached physically or their parents have died. Yet they report a continuing emotional attachment to that family, maintained by a sense of having ultimately failed to make things right, recognition of a lifetime of loss and deprivation, or a longing for an ideal parent and the childhood that was missed. All group members report difficulties in forming primary attachments of their own and severe problems with intimacy and trust.

For all of these individuals, the decision to join is triggered by a recognition that they are stuck. They cannot proceed with their own adult lives because they cannot leave their alcoholic families of origin behind. They have always felt responsible and cannot now break free.

Judy was having troubles with her studies because she couldn't concentrate. She was preoccupied with the welfare of her family and could not devote herself fully to any other goal. She had long been a parent to her younger siblings and derived her main sense of worth from this responsibility. With tremendous guilt and sadness, Judy came to therapy because she needed help to "get out of my family."

The labeling and the decision to join involve many paradoxes. Chief among these is the question of whether joining will permit a separation or intensify the attachment. Members feel the decision as an abandonment, yet recognize that they will intensify their attachment at the same time. While feeling orphaned, they wonder whether, by breaking their denial, they must become more responsible and confront their parents. Must they now work harder to make things right? Most join feeling both sides intensely.

Margaret says that to break denial is to accept responsibility for making everyone better or to make herself alone, neither choice an attractive one. She felt guilty growing up and leaving home because she was leaving chaos behind. Yet she can also blame her mother's drinking for her own problems and eventually leave because of it. Margaret summarizes her dilemma simply, saying "You cannot leave and you cannot go home."

Group members willingly place themselves in the position of awakening years of the past with the express desire of wanting to leave it. Much of the work of the group involves a regression in the transference to group members, and intensification of family attachments, moving toward ultimate emotional separation. Those who join have all realized that they could not achieve a true separation and a sense of their own independent identities by simply forgetting their past or willing themselves to be different.

Transference Implications Of The Decision To Join

Since the beginning of our program, we have marveled at the low drop-out rate and the speed at which the group develops into a cohesive, hard-working network. We have also marveled at the speed with which transference develops. Because of the importance of labeling and the issues of abandonment and betrayal presented above, the group is important to members before they get there.

> Mary Ann reported in her initial interview that she had read about the work at Stanford and carried the article bunched up in her purse for over a year. Then she spent six months on the waiting list. On the first day she joined, she noted how much the group seemed like a family and how much she wanted to belong. Weeks later she recognized that she had embraced this "family" to replace the one she was betraying.

The transference is also hastened by the label "children of alcoholics." When offered an alternative group rather than the waiting list, these individuals unanimously refuse, emphasizing the importance of being able to see themselves as children, many for the first time. The label gives them permission and thereby facilitates regression without undue guilt. They want group peers who are the children of alcoholics as well.

> Dan noted that all his efforts as a child to break the family denial had been met with greater denial and charges that what he saw and heard were inaccurate. Furthermore, he was selfish and ungrateful for saying such things about his father. Dan joined the group to try to break denial once again, to make real his past, and to have his memories and perceptions validated by others.

In a new group, or when a new member joins, members first want to know which parent was alcoholic. Next, did the alcoholic parent ever get sober, is he or she living and, often indirectly, is the newcomer concerned about his or her own alcohol use? The mandate and permission to go back and say what really happened paves the way for quick and intensive bonding based on shared experiences, the validation of perceptions and identification.

In the beginning, members who need to identify as children tend to invest the group and the leaders with an idealized positive transference. They hope the leaders will provide models of good parents and the group will be the close and supportive family they never had. This wish, as well as the idealized transference, is immediately vulnerable to the intense ambivalent and negative transference distortions which they experience in the group.

The idea of experiencing oneself as a child is not tolerable to all members. For some it brings up all too quickly intense feelings of need and deprivation and the recognition that they had to take care of themselves or starve. For many, being a child carried nothing but fear and feelings of helplessness. It was better to grow up fast. The promise of regression is experienced as a terrifying loss of control. As one member who could not stand her dependent feelings put it:

> Feeling needy in this group makes me too visible. And being that needy and that visible is like being a drunken parent.

Later, when describing the chaos and violence of her childhood, and the predominance of her parents' needs, she said simply: "How can you complain your old shoes don't fit anymore?"

The Early Phase Of The Group

Many of the same issues critical to the process of deciding to join continue as central themes in the formative stage of the new group. Identification through the sharing of experiences particularly related to alcohol, bonding by the acquisition of the label ACA, and the breakdown of denial are central. Members establish a working culture that includes a mix of suggestions for real-life issues such as visits home to drinking or sober alcoholic parents, mutual support for the breakdown of denial and the exploration of transference phenomena occurring in the group. The importance of denial, a key issue for all members of the group, illustrates the often parallel nature of these processes.

The Breakdown Of Denial

Denial is central to the defensive system of the alcoholic family. It dictates what can be "known" as well as what can be said within the family. In the ACA group, where multiple family transferences, identifications and defenses are re-enacted, it is essential to focus on the defensive aspects of denial as transference resistance. The group as a reconstituted family magnifies the intensity of transference distortions at the same time the group (family) resistance to breaking denial decreases the members' ability to confront or interpret the defense.

A member planning a visit home experienced for several weeks beforehand an increasing fear about the visit and guilt and detachment in the group. She received advice from others about how to avoid being "sucked into the vacuum," yet nothing eased her continuing discomfort. Finally, she noted that she was perplexed about her inability to say out loud what is really happening to her and her family and specifically to tell her father to keep his hands off of her. Another member nodded with complete understanding. She suggested that for Diana to verbalize her feelings and perceptions would equal the collapse of the family. Any comment about what is happening brings the pretended level of relationship and the real level too close and is too threatening. All members nodded their obvious agreement. To offer support, Henry gave the following example:

> Henry described his father dying in the hospital of cirrhosis, with members of his family standing at the foot of the bed holding their smuggled-in gin and tonics. Henry was amazed and attempted to discuss the inappropriateness of this with his

brother. The latter responded with intense hostility, telling Henry that he had said too much, transcending the rules about what could be talked about. Henry re-learned that such open discussion of drinking would not be tolerated. In the group, the individuals then began to question what was real and what wasn't and whether their discomfort was warranted.

These interactions about denial focused mainly on outside real-life issues or mutual support. However, the family transference was also activated. On the day before she was to go home, Diana sat crouched in her chair, wrapped in her buttoned coat. Members finally noted how frightened she appeared and how silent she had been. It was only then that she explored her denial and her inability to confront her parents. At the same time, she had been unable to tell the group what she was seeing and feeling with them. In later weeks, it became clear that her buttoned coat was her protection against the verbal and physical abuse she expected would occur in the group. There was continual violence in her family. Coming to the group each week awakened these fears and she had to protect herself.

Members ultimately see that breaking their denial carries with it a profound recognition of loss and isolation. Henry and Sally explored these aspects in detail. Sally's father was the alcoholic who committed suicide when she was 13. Until that time, her whole childhood was spent worrying about him. He was always at the emotional center of everything, draining everyone, with no idea of the havoc he created. They moved every year to get a fresh start and hopefully a new, improved family image. To no avail. Sally finally left her home and family to escape the "craziness."

As she described her family, the central theme was her break in denial. Yet she and Henry observed sadly that the more they acknowledged the realities in their families, the more they went against them and the more isolated they felt. Both described themselves as orphans, having authored their own abandonment by breaking their denial in order to change.

Henry illustrated this dilemma and the profound sense of loss. Both of his parents became alcoholic when he was 13. Before that time he recalls a warm, loving family. Since then, he described a constant underlying sense of expectation, hope and repeated disappointment. He could never rely on his parents to be parents to the children or to provide love and care. Both parents are now dead — from alcoholism. Henry did everything he possibly could to convince them to stop drinking. His father had been told he would die, but Henry never gave up hoping that his father would stop drinking. He did stop on several occasions and Henry became excited, thinking his father had "licked" the problem and would again be available to him. He was overwhelmed with disappointment when his father started drinking again.

> As this meeting progressed, Sally spoke with matter-of-fact determination: She had been used and was "closing the door" on her family. There was no loss for her because she had never had anything to begin with. Henry spoke softly in contrast, saying how much he wanted to belong to his family and how they were lost to him.

Henry's sense of himself as an orphan and his intense need to feel a sense of belonging resulted in a rapid transference in the group. He was extremely active eliciting information from others to speed up the processes of identification. After several weeks, the group members resisted, feeling he was pushing too fast for a sense of intimacy. Henry was frustrated and angry that the group members were demonstrating so much concern for their "personal limits." Another member quickly interpreted the transference: Henry was working hard to "bring the group together" just like he had with his family. For several weeks following this interpretation, Henry was silent and very depressed. If he could not bring this family together, what place was there for him?

The Importance Of Belonging

The theme of belonging is tied to denial and the issue of alcoholism. While on her visit, Diana wrote a letter to the group. Missing a week and being home in her alcoholic family caused her to realize that she wanted very much to belong to the group. The letter established a place for her and her wish not to be forgotten in her absence. She later recognized that it also served to help her maintain her detachment from her family while physically present with them. She tried to be an observer, to force herself to see what she had so long denied.

For many years Diana was the family problem. She was the alcoholic, the pill-popper and the uncontrollable one. Now she took part in a family dinner in which her father drank heavily for most of the day and could not prepare the meal. There was chaos, an accidental fire, and when dinner was finally served late at night, her father asked whether she objected to wine being served. Group members laughed heartily at the irony of her father's acknowledgment of her alcoholism and her recovery.

Several members now commented on the fact that their parents' alcoholism was never a permissible subject for discussion. But Margaret had the opposite experience. All kinds of people from the minister to neighbors would call her suggesting she should do something about her parents. She would have serious discussions with both parents about her mother's drinking with no change. Her mother welcomed the opportunity to talk about all the problems which caused her to drink too much, yet she maintained at the same time that she did not drink too much.

This discussion led members to the question of whether or not they belonged to their families. This question of what it means to be in or to be out of the family is often reflected in the transference in the early phase of the group. As Margaret noted,

"If you are responsible and belong, you go whenever you are called and you attempt to meet everyone's needs without question. In order to maintain the family denial, you must hold the same beliefs and attitudes as everyone else."

The risk involved in the early months of the group in challenging each others' perceptions, being angry, expressing any feeling that is different or confronting denial is only partially offset by their sad understanding that to belong to their family is to go down with them.

> Harvey always felt his wish to have different attitudes and beliefs was a betrayal of his mother (not an alcoholic). She was a resentful woman, resigned to the fact that the world had dealt her a bad hand, including her alcoholic husband. For Harvey to refuse to "inherit" that same belief system was equal to abandoning her.

Others reported that their parents expected them to agree with all their complaints, resentments and problems. It was their designated role in the family to maintain the bitter stance against an unfair world. To hold positive attitudes was equal to not belonging.

Members of this group had all acknowledged concern about their own drinking in previous weeks and now one summarized:

> To become an alcoholic is one way of not being different, or not betraying or deserting the family. It is the one clear way to belong.

Henry now added to his story, told several weeks previously, about his father's death.

> At the wake, Henry got very drunk and engaged in several foolish, dangerous acts. The next day he and his brothers (both alcoholics) shared the antics of the day before, laughing at his behavior. Henry said grimly and with sadness: "Drinking validates my membership in my family."

Shirley also illustrates the issue of belonging and the significance that membership in the group has for her in her current relationship with her family.

Shirley was reluctant and frightened to join the group. She recognized that her parents were probably alcoholic but she did not want them to be. If they were alcoholic, she would have to become responsible for them and she wanted them to be able to take care of themselves. It was only their advancing age and the recognition that she might have to "take over" anyway that prompted her to seek help. For weeks in the group, she felt like an outsider. She had always loved her parents and felt she had a "normal" good childhood and family life. She did not want this image disturbed. She wondered constantly whether being in the group meant she would have to reject her parents. She did not want to belong if that were the case, yet she knew she needed help and could no longer deny the alcoholic reality.

> Shirley solved the problem. She advised the group that she had pulled out old family albums and "reframed" pictures of her mother and father which were now sitting on her bureau. She was joining the group, not to reject her parents, but to "reframe" them. She needed to break *her* denial of the way things really were. She did not have to become responsible for them or change them.

Being Alcoholic

The meaning of being alcoholic and concern about inevitably becoming alcoholic are profoundly important issues which appear in different forms throughout the life of the group. In the early phases of the group, discussions of alcoholism are closely connected to important themes of identification, belonging and acceptance, and denial and control. Because the group has become a substitute family, the transference implications are of critical importance as are the real concerns members have about their own drinking. Denial and ambivalence are both important determinants of how these issues will be handled by individual members and by the group as a whole. Continuing ambivalence about belonging to the group is illustrated by Chuck and directly relates to the issue of his own alcoholism. Chuck noted that his parents presented nothing but extremes: His father was a serious alcoholic and his mother didn't drink at all. Chuck was constantly trying to find a middle ground so he could maintain his identification with both parents. Not having an internal sense of the middle ground, nor of appropriate limits, he was constantly looking for someone outside himself to define what is appropriate. He felt very isolated but was afraid to be like his mother or his father. He focused all his energy on being a "moderate" drinker.

> Chuck recounted that until several months ago, he had been living his life as though it were completely pre-determined and he had no choices. When told by a friend that he had a problem with alcohol, he was devastated. He suddenly became aware that the course of his life and close identification with his father and father's three brothers (all alcoholics) might make it inevitable for him too.

The lack of power, of choice, and his inability to make moderate decisions in all areas of his life seemed inevitable too. Chuck was distraught most of the time and caught in a painful dilemma. To stop drinking was to reject an identification with his father. To keep drinking was to risk being an alcoholic without choices and was a rejection of his mother.

In the group, Chuck was tense, constantly looking for rules and always demonstrating his wish to belong and not to belong at the same time. For the year that Chuck was a member of the group he was always in danger of having to leave because of a work conflict. In this way, he maintained one foot out the door. This was an irritation to others, but not nearly so much as his behavior in the group. It was impossible for him to take a stance or state an opinion. Whatever he said, he negated in the next sentence. The importance of a middle ground for Chuck resulted in no ground, no identification and no feeling of belonging. To allow himself these required an active decision about his own drinking that he could not make.

The matter of identification with and separation from one's family is reflected repeatedly in the degree to which members feel they can hope to be different from their parents. Chuck was horrified to be told he sounded like his father on the telephone. Diana put great care into her appearance as a way of dis-identifying with her mother whom she described as unkempt and sloppy. Diana said offhandedly that there was so much chaos in her family there was no time to learn about personal hygiene. Ironically, one of the ways in which members try hardest to be different is to be able to drink in a controlled, moderate way.

Alcohol, whether group members are alcoholic or not, is an important group issue for all. Harvey acknowledged it is a difficult and uncomfortable subject for him. His whole life was connected to alcohol in a very positive way. He recalled going with his idolized and now idealized father to the corner bar, sharing memorable father-son encounters in this atmosphere.

> Being able to drink and control it is tied to Harvey's self-esteem and his masculinity. If he had to stop, it would be equal to saying that the booze had control over him and that was unacceptable. Until deciding to join the group, he never considered that his father didn't have control over the booze either.

The matter of control and its relation to alcohol is always a primary issue. It is reflected in the early group as a wish for rules, and constant uncertainty about what is the "right amount" to reveal, who sets limits, and what is appropriate behavior at any given time. As we learned early in our work (Cermak and Brown, 1982), members equate the experience of feeling, and particularly of feeling out of control — feeling too happy, too sad, revealing too much — to being drunk.

The development of family transference in the group is not dependent on members working openly on their own drinking concerns. Intense reactions and distortions arise in response to sustained emotional outbursts on the part of a member. unpredictability, expressions of anger, and often to confusion and ambivalence. One or more members, and occasionally the entire group, will react as though they were attempting to get a drunk parent calmed down and back under control. Conversely, silence, with-drawal or critical comments are often reacted to as though they are being communicated by a sober, depressed and/or critical, angry parent. Although these are transference reactions, the behavior which evokes the reaction is often a startlingly accurate re-creation of the parents' behavior. The member responding to this communication is reacting to very real and familiar behavior in the present with intense feelings developed in the family in the past.

Linda, who does not drink, was raised by a single parent, her alcoholic mother. She is very emotional and identified with her mother's drunken style of communication, which was confused and rambling. Pat, who is depressed and often silent in the group, exerts a tremendous amount of control over Linda through her body language and disap-proving facial expressions. Eventually Pat was able to say:

> I feel hopeless about being able to help you. You're just like my father (an alcoholic), and your upsetness keeps you from doing anything to make your life better. We've been through all this before and it hasn't done any good.

It is interesting to note that "upsetness" is the euphe-mism used by Pat's mother to explain her father's chronic and severe alcoholism. Linda's emotionality sets off feelings of hopelessness and anger in Pat and she expresses it through the depression and withdrawal that her mother used towards her father.

The adult child of an alcoholic who is also an alcoholic has some special problems and fears to deal with in the group, especially in the early months of recovery. Uncov-ering repressed memories and feelings too rapidly can trigger a drinking bout — to treat the guilt or to slow the uncovering process. The rapid uncovering process and the erosion of denial, personal and familial, can be extremely frightening. Careful individual evaluations before the group begins allow for a delayed entry into the group so that new defenses needed to maintain sobriety can be more solidly established.

In the formative stage of the group, it is clear that denial, belonging and the meaning of being alcoholic are critical themes. Each is directly related to the family of origin and fraught with conflict. As the many examples illustrate, members all maintain a primary though ambivalent attachment to their alcoholic families of origin. As one member put it poignantly: "I need a family I can come from and belong to." For most, the group has become the object of this wish and as the involvement and commitment is firmly established and the level of work deepens, the transference becomes more intense.

Ongoing Group Work: Intensification Of The Transference

With the passage of time and the development of a cohesive, supportive group culture, the focus shifts. There is less sharing of factual information about the history of their families and therefore less identification through shared experience. There is less advice about dealing with real-life issues and more attention to the interactions occurring within the group in the "here-and-now" (Yalom, 1975). Because of the speed of identification and cohesion, the move toward in-depth group work occurs quite rapidly. Even so, the three levels, advice and identification, the breakdown of denial about the past and present, and exploration of the transference, are always coexistent. The issue of alcoholism remains a central core. In contrast to the early emphasis on denial and belonging, central themes revolve around dependability, predictability, the challenge of deep perceptions about oneself and the family, and the repeated questioning of whether their parents cared for them. These are often worked out transferentially among group members.

Predictability And Dependability

The issues of predictability and dependability are reflected repeatedly as the group members deepen their commitment to the process of uncovering.

Many group members share a continuing feeling of impending disaster about the group. It was often experienced as a vague, overriding anxiety that never diminished regardless of what occurred in the meeting. Members related this feeling back to their alcoholic families in which they felt responsible to carry the burden of an "impending catastrophe," always on guard and responsible for a family out of control: a drunken parent, a violent parent, a critical demanding parent, an unavailable parent. One member mistakenly arrived early for the group and found no one present. He suffered acute panic and an immediate reawakening of deep feelings of fear and loss. As a child, he often arrived home to an empty house, never certain whether his parents were safe and when they would arrive home.

Another member, absolutely terrified each week before coming, said she could not risk deepening her feelings of need and attachment to the others when they might not show up, an experience she encountered frequently with her family.

At another meeting following the departure of a popular, active member, others were quiet, refusing to engage one another or explore their feelings of fear and loss. For the entire meeting members examined whether it was worth it to risk caring about others and oneself and to risk feeling dependent on the group, when members could leave. In this context, members compared their feelings to those of abandonment they experienced repeatedly when a parent got drunk. They could never count on the sustained attention of their parents and therefore could never wholly let themselves feel the depth of their needs for someone to listen and to take care of them.

All maintained that they had survived their childhood by *not* needing anyone.

> Sam described himself as the "boy wonder" — bright, science student, invested in his study and the care of his sisters; he maintained with pride that he needed no help with anything.

Most members agreed that they feel safe only when alone; otherwise, they must be on the lookout for a disaster which they must survive and try to fix.

Tied to the sense of impending calamity is a deep feeling of responsibility for their parents. Members speak in the group as parents who have failed. They recognize their inability to set limits on the needs and demands of others and trace it back to their families. This persistent sense of helplessness and failure is often poignantly demonstrated as the painful affect is experienced in a here-and-now interaction in the group.

> Margaret was anxious and frustrated because of her inability to make things better for Sally. As the latter broke into tears one day, Margaret cried too. When asked why she was crying with Sally, Margaret recalled feeling continually unable to make her mother feel better. She often sat beside her tearful mother on the bed and cried with her.

As Margaret traced this painful memory and experienced the depth of her feelings of helplessness in the group, she recounted her recognition of her difficulty in accepting the limits of her ability to help others. As she grew up, she consciously tried to give up the idea that she could meet her mother's needs. Her mother demonstrated that this was impossible by being drunk, out of reach and out of control. In the immediacy of the group the unconscious, dynamic response reveals the deep need to be a "good enough" mother to her mother and the sadness at her inability to do so.

The matter of predictability was related to control in a very important ongoing way for one member. At the start of the group, the male co-therapist wore long hair and casual attire. This pleased Dan, a graduate student who projected a struggle with authority onto the therapist and identified with him as a student (the therapist was a resident in training). Dan was shocked when Tim appeared one day wearing a suit and tie, with his hair cut short. Dan felt betrayed and abandoned by Tim's change in appearance. The matter of dress now became a steady, significant theme, particularly when Tim changed back and forth from casual to more formal attire.

Dan was surprised to see Tim in his former dress and wondered why Tim would change back since the group approved of his newer "garb." It seemed to Dan that Tim's choice of dress reflects the way he feels about himself and what he wishes to communicate. Dan wants to believe there is only one way to feel and think and therefore only one way to dress. Tim's "experimentation" with different styles means a lack of control and is very threatening. More importantly, Tim's change in appearance is a deviation from what Dan has come to expect and therefore challenges his security based on Tim's predictability.

The shifts in dress (more than the actual outfits) were directly related to unpredictable states of drunkenness. With two radically different "looks" Tim now represented a changing drunk or sober father.

Dan wanted to be able to rely on Tim and could not, if Tim could so readily change his appearance. He recalled repeatedly the sudden loss of his father to an alcoholic binge.

On another level, Dan was perplexed that Tim could risk trying anything new without prior knowledge of the consequences. He marveled that Tim might experiment with "being out of control" and manage it so well. When he thought about experimenting himself, Dan could only picture himself out of control, a "bull in a china shop."

Deeper levels of transference directed towards the therapists are not often risked in the early phase of the group. Although this material emerges among the members of the group, intense fears as well as hostile and aggressive transference toward the therapist are often warded off or neutralized. In the ongoing work of the long-term ACA group, the therapists become more viable transference figures for the repetition of specific disturbing patterns which originated early in the members' alcoholic families.

The focus on predictability reappears in many guises, particularly around the issue of separation and major changes in the group. In an advanced group, the female co-therapist became pregnant. Members experienced this news as a significant anticipated loss and dealt with many feelings of jealousy, rivalry and abandonment. The therapist took a leave of absence of several months and unfortunately was not able to set a firm date of return due to personal circumstances.

When she did return, members expressed a variety of reactions to her departure but especially to the unpredictable return. Several took it for granted that she would never be back. Early in their lives they had learned they couldn't count on parents so they simply didn't try. She was gone and would not be back. They felt nothing — no anger, no loss and no need. But several others were enraged. These women had alcoholic mothers who unpredictably but regularly got drunk, leaving them to care for the family.

During her absence, both women felt extremely anxious and responsible for holding the group together. In their view, the male therapist was unavailable, unresponsive and inadequate to running the group. With intense anger, one of these women yelled at the therapist: "You left us responsible! You were drunk!" Months later the other recalled the anxiety of that period in the group and the constant fear and anxiety in her family. She stammered, unable to remember the therapist's name as she finally blurted out: "What could we expect from you! You were passed out!"

The group stuck with these issues for several weeks. Both of these women, active during the therapist's absence, now became quiet. Soon one realized that it was her duty in the family to be in charge, to hold the family together, but to make it look like her mother was actually presiding. She now had to maintain this charade in the group.

The Challenge To Deep Perceptions

Members expect that much of the group's work will involve the re-creation of their families. Despite this recognition, members of an older group rejected the notion of transference when presented to them at a deeper level in relation to the therapists. To acknowledge any perception of the therapists as parental figures was to lose them — to feel alone, unprotected and uncared for. Ben illustrates the development of this awareness.

For months he insisted that he saw the therapists quite positively as peers with whom he could share the deep feelings of loss and deprivation he experienced with his real parents. Ben typically spoke in a monotone, conveying an overriding sense of hopelessness and depression. He felt involved in the group and was dismayed and hurt that members forgot what he said and seemed not to hear what was important to him. His depression deepened. The issue finally crystallized in relation to Tim, the male therapist.

> Ben had steadfastly maintained that Tim represented to him a caring brother. To see Tim as a father figure (with the female therapist as a mother) was to give up hope of receiving anything. To see either as a parent was to automatically orphan and isolate himself.
>
> One day Ben arrived and angrily asked why something important he had said had been left out of the summary. How could he be so unimportant? Ben directed his anger toward Tim. Recalling events in the group and in writing the summary, the therapist realized that he had focused on something that involved himself, leaving out Ben's important comments. This was evidence to Ben that Tim's needs were more important, that he couldn't be counted on, and most importantly, that Tim didn't care. Now, he recognized the relation to his family. The needs of his alcoholic father were always first. He felt uncared for, unimportant and alone.

The therapist was able to acknowledge that his own needs had indeed colored his perceptions and reporting but he challenged Ben's belief that this meant he didn't care. Over several weeks Ben tinkered with the notion that Tim's needs could be dominant and he could still care at the same time. He accepted this possibility and experienced a major shift in his relationships in the group and with his family.

> If the therapist could care for him, then maybe his father did too, even though his own needs were so great and he was

so often drunk and unavailable. This recognition allowed Ben to hope for the first time in many years and opened the way for him to feel his longing, which he had denied by refusing to see the group as a family.

Subsequently, Ben visited his real family and opened a new relationship with his father, now sober. Obviously such a happy ending is not possible nor necessarily desirable for many or even most. In Ben's case the fact that his father was now sober and he could make contact is unusual. What is most important and what occurs more often is the shift in a deeply held perception expressed in the intensity of the parental transference and worked through in the group. It was Ben's recognition that his father could have cared for him that gave him hope. This shift comes for many regardless of the real parental behavior in the past or present.

Jack illustrates this process in relation to his persistent negative transference to the male co-therapist. Jack had great difficulty relating to two co-therapists. He directed his positive feelings and attention toward the female, ignoring or belittling the male with contemptuous remarks. While the pattern was consistent, the meanings were not clear until the female therapist was absent. On that day, Jack felt much more positively about the male, an experience he had never had in his family.

Jack recognized that he had sided with his divorced mother against his alcoholic father. He adopted her feelings of contempt for him and her belief that his father was a drunken bum who cared for him not at all. Jack used to visit his father in the bar, be aggressively obnoxious with him and then accept a payoff from his father to leave.

Jack was repeatedly obnoxious toward Tim in the group, hoping that Tim would become angry, show himself as crass and rejecting and ultimately kick him out of the group.

Jack realized that he had no experience living with two parents and could only operate pitting one against the other. Following his time alone with Tim, he dramatically shifted his behavior and perceptions, now exploring the possibility that maybe his father cared for him after all. In this context, Jack recognized his deep need for his father and his long "secret attachment" to him. In bitter, angry moments with his mother, he still reminds her with great hostility of his own alcoholism (he is a sober alcoholic) to accent how much he is like his father.

Over the next few weeks in the group Jack's positive feelings toward Tim grew in direct proportion to his increasing negative feelings toward Stephanie. He began to see her as critical, judgmental and diminishing of her male co-therapist, whom he now heard as very supportive. In time, the working through of this splitting in the transference should allow Jack to integrate the positive and negative aspects of his feelings toward both therapists as well as his parents.

Another member of this group provides a final illustration regarding parental transference in the group, accenting the critical importance of alcohol in relation to whether her parents care.

Betsy worked readily with the female therapist on her relationship with her mother (the alcoholic). It was clear that her relationship to her father was also problematic, but she could not approach it in the group. She felt contemptuous of Tim or so anxious in his presence that she could not remember his name. She described her own father as unavailable, confusing, inadequate in caring for his children and unprotective of her with her abusive alcoholic mother.

With over two years in the group, Betsy finally recognized that her father was an alcoholic too. This breakdown in her firm denial released a flood of deep feelings of helplessness, loneliness and terror. She had survived by holding onto the belief that her father would protect her and rescue her from her mother. She now recognized that they drank together and that he was an alcoholic too. She had to abandon the myth that he would ultimately rescue her and re-experience the complete and utter helplessness she felt as a child.

From her entry into the group, Betsy experienced one serious crisis after another, from illness to accidents to being the victim of an armed robbery. In the group, members tolerated Betsy's long despair. Yet she repeatedly attacked the others for needing her to feel better. She recalled that her alcoholic parents had needed her to validate their worth as parents. Yet they did not provide the care and protection she so desperately needed. Over the course of two and a half years, Betsy experienced two co-therapists and group members who cared and who were available and dependable through many crises. Her real family did not change.

Termination

As with the decision to join the group, the decision to leave is full of personal meaning and directly related to resolved and unresolved issues in the alcoholic family. The adult children of alcoholics are particularly sensitive to separation and abandonment. The termination process for any member triggers the emergence of these issues in the transference as well as in the defense against experiencing painful and/or repressed feelings of loss and bereavement. As Yalom points out (1975), "Termination is more than an extraneous event in the group; it is the microcosmic representation of some of the most crucial and painful issues of all."

In this final section we will discuss some of these issues as well as more general problems dealt with in instances where a member drops out shortly after joining the group and in early terminations.

Drop-Outs

Very few of our members drop out, leaving early and unsuccessfully. Those who do have found the breakdown in denial and the perceived betrayal of their parents intolerable. For some it is the problem of focusing on their own early recovery and the need to make this focus a priority which leads to dropping out of the ACA group. Matt illustrates these issues.

Matt was the only son of two active alcoholic parents. Matt was concerned about his own drinking as a primary problem as well on entering the group. He felt pushed into treatment because his marriage was breaking up, due in large part to his wife's complaints about his drinking.

Matt joined the group with the agreement that he would consider his own drinking a priority problem and seek help for it in addition to his group work.

From his entrance, Matt's attendance was irregular and he was frequently tardy. Members were quick to point out his resistance to joining and encouraged him to discuss his conflicts. Following the several occasions during which he was active and involved, he was absent, or quiet, feeling tremendous guilt about his participation. Ultimately, his sense of betrayal of his family and the recognition of his own alcoholism were intolerable. He could not accept the emotional break from his family which he perceived membership required. Matt terminated after three months, acknowledging that he was not ready to make the commitment.

One young woman had been close to her mother throughout the latter's recovery, had taken part in family therapy as part of her mother's alcohol treatment program and firmly believed that her support and acceptance were a crucial part of her mother's sobriety. She was deeply disturbed as other members of the group began to explore their anger and disappointments in regard to their own alcoholic parents. These explorations threatened to make her aware of her own anger toward her mother, and the fear she felt at the possible separation and growth away from her mother. She experienced intense anxiety which made the meetings intolerable.

Careful initial evaluations as well as attention to individual process in the early weeks of the group help to reduce drop-outs as well as to anticipate problems that some individuals may experience once they have joined the group.

Early Termination

A number of group members leave early, though they are not drop-outs, unsuccessful or casualties. For most, outside circumstances have dictated a premature departure. Several Stanford students have graduated and moved away, for example.

Others used their work in the group as a springboard for changes outside. Following a year of important work in the group one member intentionally left a public, politically stressful position, moving to a rural area and a new career. A very important and positive move, it was nevertheless premature in terms of his work in the group.

Others have left early because the anxiety of the uncovering process is too great. Chuck and Diana, described above, are examples. Each was committed to the group and hard-working for many months. The breakdown in denial and the too-rapid uncovering process became intolerable. Chuck could no longer stay in the group and maintain his "middle" position. To him, the group represented a commitment to an extreme. But to move, to take a stand, was impossible.

Diana became too frightened at the realities she was discovering about herself and her family. It was too much too fast and she needed to slow herself down.

Appropriate Termination

A number of our members have remained in the group to the point of appropriate termination. It is quite clear to us now that there are several key experiences essential to this completion.

Examination of the progress of these members reveals that the life history of the group represents three key phases: growing up, growing out and coming home. Members break their own denial about the past, recalling their childhood and growing up days as they really were. In the group, the experience of themselves as children awakens these memories and facilitates regression and family transference.

"Growing out" is the process of detachment from the active need to protect and save the alcoholic or other family members. It is the difficult and painful relinquishment of defenses that serve the ACA well: the fixer, the responsible one, the comic, the alcoholic, the problem. It is the recognition of limits and the deflation of grandiosity and omnipotence. In the group, members work through these defenses and the distortions they generate, slowly recognizing that they cannot control each other, just as they could not control or "make well" their parents. As Margaret could begin to see with her mother:

> She lets me know I can do nothing, by being out of reach, out of control and drunk.

The key for all members is in "coming home." Following detachment and separation is the return. Each member approaching full and appropriate termination has made this return in some way, not necessarily directly or in person. It is a confrontation in which the member breaks the denial, tells the family secret and "makes real the past."

As illustrated above, Ben's deepest perceptions about his family were challenged as they emerged in the transference to the male therapist. In time he was able to shift these perceptions about his family and reopened his relationship with them.

Betsy considered leaving the group on several occasions but recognized that something was unfinished. It scared her to continue, but she remained. Following her recognition that her father was *also* an alcoholic and the crushing of her rescue fantasy, she approached her father by telephone.

> No longer would she participate in all the family secrets and no longer would she try so hard to fix everyone up. And furthermore, she recited her knowledge of past events which she and the family had carefully hidden for many years.

Following her confrontation, Betsy experienced a freedom unknown to her. She felt accepting about her mother and her father and about her inability to make them well. She detached further and further from her active need to rescue them and moved ahead in her own relationships and career development.

Eileen, 60 years old and a recovering alcoholic member of the group for three and a half years, illustrates this process quite well. Her feelings about her father and his alcoholism were a deep shadow to her, unknown but causing her regular pain. She believed deeply that her father never cared for her and she felt only anger, hurt and hatred toward him. Prior to her termination, Eileen had a dream in which she was a young woman speaking to her father, also much younger (actually dead for over 30 years), in the truthful, open and direct manner she always wished for. In the dream, she told her father exactly how she felt about his alcoholism and what she had missed getting from him because of it. In this encounter her father listened and seemed to hear her, accepting her needs and wishes and the validity of her point of view. Following this dream, Eileen moved rapidly toward termination.

As she approached departure from the group, she recognized that a major achievement was her increasing comfort with multiple and contradictory emotions, both in the present and the past. In recognizing that her father could have cared for her, she opened the door to forgive him. Instead of profoundly negative emotions, she now developed a more complex portrait of her father, including both positive and negative feelings.

The process of re-interpreting the past as it is repeated in the present context of the group, relinquishing fantasies of omnipotence as well as impotence, and integrating insight and experience in a way that permits effective interpersonal relationships are the rewards of the difficult and painful work done in the ACA group. They are also the markers that inform both therapist and member when an individual is appropriately ready to terminate.

References

1. Cermak, T., and Brown, S., "Interactional group therapy with the adult children of alcoholics," in *International Journal of Group Psychotherapy*, 32:3, 1982.

2. Beletsis, S., and Brown, S., "A developmental framework for understanding the adult children of alcoholics," in *Focus on Women, Journal of Addictions and Health*, 187-203, 1981.

3. Yalom, I., Brown, S., and Bloch, S., "The written summary as a group psychotherapy technique," in *Archives of General Psychiatry*, 32:5, 605-618, 1975.

4. Black, C., **It Will Never Happen To Me.** Denver: M.A.C. Printing and Publications, 1981.

5. Wegscheider, S., **Another Chance: Hope And Help For The Alcoholic Family.** Palo Alto: Science and Behavior Books, 1981.

6. El-Guebaly, N., and Offord, D.R., in "The offspring of alcoholics: A clinical review," in *The American Journal of Psychiatry*, 134:4, 357-365, 1977.

7. _____ "On being the offspring of an alcoholic: an update," in *Alcoholism: Clinical and Experimental Research*, Vol. 3, 148-157, 1979.

Helpful 12-Step Books from . . .
Health Communications

HEALING A BROKEN HEART:
12 Steps of Recovery for Adult Children
Kathleen W.
This useful 12-Step book is presently the number one resource for all
Adult Children support groups.
ISBN 0-932194-65-6 $7.95

12 STEPS TO SELF-PARENTING For Adult Children
Philip Oliver-Diaz and Patricia A. O'Gorman
This gentle 12-Step guide takes the reader from pain to healing and self-
parenting, from anger to forgiveness, and from fear and despair to
recovery.
ISBN 0-932194-68-0 $7.95

THE 12-STEP STORY BOOKLETS
Mary M. McKee
Each beautifully illustrated booklet deals with a step, using a story from
nature in parable form. The 12 booklets (one for each step) lead us to a
better understanding of ourselves and our recovery.
ISBN 1-55874-002-3 $8.95

WITH GENTLENESS, HUMOR AND LOVE:
A 12-Step Guide for Adult Children in Recovery
Kathleen W. and Jewell E.
Focusing on adult child issues such as reparenting the inner child, self-
esteem, intimacy and feelings, this well-organized workbook teaches
techniques and tools for the 12-step recovery programs.
ISBN 0-932194-77-X $7.95

GIFTS FOR PERSONAL GROWTH & RECOVERY
Wayne Kritsberg
A goldmine of positive techniques for recovery (affirmations, journal
writing, visualizations, guided meditations, etc.), this book is indispens-
able for those seeking personal growth.
ISBN 0-932194-60-5 $6.95

Enterprise Center, 3201 S.W. 15th Street,
Deerfield Beach, FL 33442
1-800-851-9100

**Health
Communications, Inc.**

Books from . . .
Health Communications

AFTER THE TEARS: Reclaiming The Personal Losses of Childhood
Jane Middelton-Moz and Lorie Dwinnel
Your lost childhood must be grieved in order for you to recapture your self-worth and enjoyment of life. This book will show you how.
ISBN 0-932194-36-2 $7.95

HEALING YOUR SEXUAL SELF
Janet Woititz
How can you break through the aftermath of sexual abuse and enter into healthy relationships? Survivors are shown how to recognize the problem and deal effectively with it.
ISBN 1-55874-018-X $7.95

RECOVERY FROM RESCUING
Jacqueline Castine
Effective psychological and spiritual principles teach you when to take charge, when to let go, and how to break the cycle of guilt and fear that keeps you in the responsibility trap. Mind-altering ideas and exercises will guide you to a more carefree life.
ISBN 1-55874-016-3 $7.95

ADDICTIVE RELATIONSHIPS: Reclaiming Your Boundaries
Joy Miller
We have given ourselves away to spouse, lover, children, friends or parents. By examining where we are, where we want to go and how to get there, we can reclaim our personal boundaries and the true love of ourselves.
ISBN 1-55874-003-1 $7.95

RECOVERY FROM CO-DEPENDENCY:
It's Never Too Late To Reclaim Your Childhood
Laurie Weiss, Jonathan B. Weiss
Having been brought up with life-repressing decisions, the adult child recognizes something isn't working. This book shows how to change decisions and live differently and fully.
ISBN 0-932194-85-0 $9.95

SHIPPING/HANDLING: All orders shipped UPS unless weight exceeds 200 lbs., special routing is requested, or delivery territory is outside continental U.S. Orders outside United States shipped either Air Parcel Post or Surface Parcel Post. Shipping and handling charges apply to all orders shipped whether UPS, Book Rate, Library Rate, Air or Surface Parcel Post or Common Carrier and will be charged as follows. Orders less than $25.00 in value add $2.00 minimum. Orders from $25.00 to $50.00 in value (after discount) add $2.50 minimum. Orders greater than $50.00 in value (after discount) add 6% of value. Orders $25.00 outside United States add 15% of value. We are not responsible for loss or damage unless material is shipped UPS. Allow 3-5 weeks after receipt of order for delivery. Prices are subject to change without prior notice.

Enterprise Center, 3201 S.W. 15th Street,
Deerfield Beach, FL 33442
1-800-851-9100

Health
Communications, Inc.

Other Books By . . .
Health Communications

ADULT CHILDREN OF ALCOHOLICS
Janet Woititz
Over a year on *The New York Times* Best-Seller list, this book is the primer on Adult Children of Alcoholics.
ISBN 0-932194-15-X $6.95

STRUGGLE FOR INTIMACY
Janet Woititz
Another best-seller, this book gives insightful advice on learning to love more fully.
ISBN 0-932194-25-7 $6.95

DAILY AFFIRMATIONS: For Adult Children of Alcoholics
Rokelle Lerner
These positive affirmations for every day of the year paint a mental picture of your life as you choose it to be.
ISBN 0-932194-27-3 $6.95

CHOICEMAKING: For Co-dependents, Adult Children and Spirituality Seekers — Sharon Wegscheider-Cruse
This useful book defines the problems and solves them in a positive way.
ISBN 0-932194-26-5 $9.95

LEARNING TO LOVE YOURSELF: Finding Your Self-Worth
Sharon Wegscheider-Cruse
"Self-worth is a choice, not a birthright," says the author as she shows us how we can choose positive self-esteem.
ISBN 0-932194-39-7 $7.95

BRADSHAW ON: THE FAMILY: A Revolutionary Way of Self-Discovery
John Bradshaw
The host of the nationally televised series of the same name shows us how families can be healed and individuals can realize full potential.
ISBN 0-932194-54-0 $9.95

HEALING THE CHILD WITHIN:
Discovery and Recovery for Adult Children of Dysfunctional Families
Charles Whitfield
Dr. Whitfield defines, describes and discovers how we can reach our Child Within to heal and nurture our woundedness.
ISBN 0-932194-40-0 $8.95

Enterprise Center, 3201 S.W. 15th Street,
Deerfield Beach, FL 33442
1-800-851-9100

Health Communications, Inc.

Daily Affirmation Books from . . .
Health Communications

GENTLE REMINDERS FOR CO-DEPENDENTS: *Daily Affirmations*
Mitzi Chandler
With insight and humor, Mitzi Chandler takes the co-dependent and the adult child through the year. Gentle Reminders is for those in recovery who seek to enjoy the miracle each day brings.
ISBN 1-55874-020-1   **$6.95**

TIME FOR JOY: *Daily Affirmations*
Ruth Fishel
With quotations, thoughts and healing energizing affirmations these daily messages address the fears and imperfections of being human, guiding us through self-acceptance to a tangible peace and the place within where there is *time for joy.*
ISBN 0-932194-82-6   **$6.95**

CRY HOPE: *Positive Affirmations For Healthy Living*
Jan Veltman
This book gives positive daily affirmations for seekers and those in recovery. Every day is a new adventure, and change is a challenge.
ISBN 0-932194-74-5   **$6.95**

SAY YES TO LIFE: *Daily Affirmations For Recovery*
Father Leo Booth
These meditations take you through the year day by day with Father Leo Booth, looking for answers and sometimes discovering that there are none. Father Leo tells us, "For the recovering compulsive person God is too important to miss — may you find Him now."
IBN 0-932194-46-X   **$6.95**

DAILY AFFIRMATIONS: *For Adult Children of Alcoholics*
Rokelle Lerner
Affirmations are a way to discover personal awareness, growth and spiritual potential, and self-regard. Reading this book gives us an opportunity to nurture ourselves, learn who we are and what we want to become.
ISBN 0-932194-47-3
(Little Red Book)   **$6.95**
(New Cover Edition)   **$6.95**

Enterprise Center, 3201 S.W. 15th Street,
Deerfield Beach, FL 33442
1-800-851-9100

Health Communications, Inc.

New Books . . .
from Health Communications

HEALING THE SHAME THAT BINDS YOU
John Bradshaw
Toxic shame is the core problem in our compulsions, co-dependencies and addictions. The author offers healing techniques to help release the shame that binds us.
ISBN 0-932194-86-9 $9.95

THE MIRACLE OF RECOVERY:
Healing For Addicts, Adult Children and Co-dependents
Sharon Wegscheider-Cruse
Beginning with recognizing oneself as a survivor, it is possible to move through risk and change to personal transformation.
ISBN 1-55874-024-4 $9.95

CHILDREN OF TRAUMA: *Rediscovering Your Discarded Self*
Jane Middelton-Moz
This beautiful book shows how to discover the source of past traumas and grieve them to grow into whole and complete adults.
ISBN 1-55874-014-7 $9.95

New Books on Spiritual Recovery . . .

LEARNING TO LIVE IN THE NOW: *6-Week Personal Plan To Recovery*
Ruth Fishel
The author gently introduces you step by step to the valuable healing tools of meditation, positive creative visualization and affirmations.
ISBN 0-932194-62-1 $7.95

CYCLES OF POWER: *A User's Guide To The Seven Seasons of Life*
Pamela Levin
This innovative book unveils the process of life as a cyclic pattern, providing strategies to use the seven seasons to regain power over your life.
ISBN 0-932194-75-3 $9.95

MESSAGES FROM ANNA: *Lessons in Living (Santa Claus, God and Love)*
Zoe Rankin
This is a quest for the meaning of "love." In a small Texas Gulf Coast town a wise 90-year-old woman named Anna shares her life messages.
ISBN 1-55874-013-9 $7.95

THE FLYING BOY: *Healing The Wounded Man*
John Lee
A man's journey to find his "true masculinity" and his way out of co-dependent and addictive relationships, this book is about feelings — losing them, finding them, expressing them.
ISBN 1-55874-006-6 $7.95

Enterprise Center, 3201 S.W. 15th Street,
Deerfield Beach, FL 33442
1-800-851-9100

Health
Communications, Inc.